GROWING PAINS

HOME TO HEATHER CREEK

GROWING PAINS

Diann Hunt

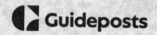

Published by Guideposts
100 Reserve Road, Suite E200
Danbury, CT 06810
Guideposts.org

Cover by Lookout Design, Inc.
Interior design by Cindy LaBreacht
Additional design work by Müllerhaus
Typeset by Aptara, Inc.

ISBN 978-1-961125-26-1 (hardcover)
ISBN 978-1-961125-28-5 (epub)

Printed in the United States of America
10 9 8 7 6 5 4 3 2

Home to Heather Creek

GROWING PAINS

Chapter One

Charlotte Stevenson shooed away a fly and wiped the perspiration from the back of her neck with a handkerchief. A strand of brown hair stuck to her cheek and she tucked it behind her ear with a sigh. She held onto the bowl of fresh green beans and kicked the porch swing into gear, hoping to stir up a breeze. The warm August air was taking its toll on her patience. She'd snapped so many green beans, she didn't know if she'd ever be able to look at another bean, let alone eat any.

"Afternoon, neighbor." Hannah Carter practically skipped up the walk toward the porch. Charlotte wondered if she'd had bounce in her step ten years ago when she was Hannah's age.

"Well, someone is mighty chipper today." Charlotte could use a good dose of Hannah's energy this Sunday afternoon.

"And for good reason," Hannah said.

Charlotte stopped snapping the beans and looked up at her best friend and neighbor of thirty years. "Oh?" It was then that she noticed the sparkle in Hannah's eyes and the grin that lit up her face like a harvest moon on a clear, autumn night.

Hannah climbed onto the porch swing with Charlotte and turned to her. Her thin frame barely rocked the swing. "You won't believe this. I still can't believe it. I never win anything."

"Believe what? Win what?" Now Charlotte's radar was on.

"You remember I told you about that drawing they were having over in Appleton for the free stay in the new bed-and-breakfast?"

"Yeah, I remember."

"I won!" Hannah jumped slightly and clapped her hands together with such vigor she almost fell off the porch swing and dumped the green beans from Charlotte's bowl.

"Oh my, that is wonderful!" Charlotte said, hanging on to the bowl for dear life. She gave her friend a congratulatory hug.

"I haven't even told you the best part yet," Hannah said, eyes still sparkling.

Her enthusiasm was contagious, spilled onto the swing, and sent tiny bumps up Charlotte's arms.

"There's more?"

"Yes. I want you to go with me." Hannah grinned.

A sharp breath caught in Charlotte's throat. Her gaze swept the farm. "But I couldn't possibly—"

"You couldn't possibly decline. This is the chance of a lifetime." Hannah had all the excitement of a schoolgirl just asked to prom.

"What about Frank?" Charlotte asked.

"I was worried about that too, what with his heart attack only two months ago. But he's getting stronger every day.

And he assures me he'll be fine. But I thought I'd ask Bob to check in on him and his sister will stop by as well," she said. "With good neighbors close by, I won't worry. Besides, he's the one who suggested you. He held his hand to his heart and told me he wasn't up for it."

Charlotte's eyes grew wide and she gave a little gasp.

"With a grin, of course. We both know the place is too frou-frou for him." Hannah chuckled.

"It does sound fun," Charlotte said, wistfully gazing across the lawn. Never in a million years could she imagine allowing herself such a luxury. She blinked and looked back to Hannah. "There's so much to do. School is about to start, the Brown family gave us all those beans and tomatoes to can for the shut-ins . . . ."

"Now, I will not take no for an answer. Why don't you get some help with that?"

"I hate to bother anyone," Charlotte said, her quick fingers once again snapping away at the beans.

"You could call a work day with the hospitality group and we could help you can the beans and tomatoes. We'd have them done in no time."

Charlotte considered the suggestion.

"But the kids? Bob? I know they can survive without me, but I hate to leave them with everything."

"Charlotte, it's for a weekend, not a month." Hannah's smile faltered, the sparkle in her eyes started to fade.

Charlotte took in the disappointment on her friend's face and mustered a smile. "You are so sweet to consider sharing such a wonderful gift with me. I'll talk it over with Bob, okay?"

Smile and sparkle zipped back into place. "Good. I'm sure Bob will want you to go."

Charlotte laughed. "Well, don't pack my clothes just yet. Let's see what he has to say." She plucked a few more beans from the bowl. "By the way, when are you going?"

"The last weekend of this month."

"Boy, that is right before school starts and all the hustle-bustle of that."

"And if I know you—and I do—you'll have everything ready to go by then."

"That's true."

Hannah seemed to have an answer for everything. Charlotte sighed. She knew they would have a great deal of fun if they went together. Their bond of friendship was like a strong rope, bound together by threads of laughing, crying, and working together in the journey of life.

"Oh, you just have to come, Charlotte. It will be such fun." Hannah rambled on with the details of the phone call she'd received and how wonderfully quaint the town of Appleton was—just the perfect getaway for two women who could use a break from the rigors of farm life.

By the time Hannah left, Charlotte found herself dreaming of the time away.

CHARLOTTE AND BOB pulled the covers down on the bed and plumped the pillows.

"I think you should go, Charlotte," Bob said. "You stood by Hannah and Frank during his recovery in the hospital. You both deserve some down time away. Not only that, but you've been dragging around here with little energy. I think the time away would do you good."

They slipped in between the cool, crisp sheets and she turned to him. "Hey, are you trying to get rid of me?"

He smiled. "You know better than that." He lifted his arm and she snuggled beneath it.

"It does sound like fun. There's just so much to do."

"There always will be—you know that. That's how it is on a farm. The work never ends. But that doesn't mean you don't take a break now and then."

"Always the voice of reason," she mumbled, breathing in the scent of fresh linens and the man she loved.

"I didn't get around to telling you today that Brad Weber stopped me after church this morning."

"Oh?"

"Seems he and the family are taking an extended trip to Montana to visit his wife's relatives."

"Is Andy able to run AA Tractor Supply alone?" she asked, referring to Brad's father, who had Parkinson's disease.

Bob chuckled. "Well, I guess that's where I come in."

Charlotte moved so she could look at Bob's face. "What does that mean?"

"Brad wants me to help Andy while he's gone."

"Really?" She scooted out of his grasp and propped herself up a little. "How do you feel about that?"

"I don't mind. It will help them out and it won't be for long. Besides, I practically know that store like the back of my hand."

"That's true." Charlotte paused a moment, wondering

how this was going to work out for Bob. "So do you think you'll do it?"

"Are you okay with that?" he asked.

"Sure. Like you said, it would be helping out our friends and it won't last forever."

"Good. Now, we'd better get some shut-eye. Brad's going to train me in the morning."

"You mean you had already made your decision?"

"Yeah." He laughed. "I knew you wouldn't care."

Charlotte chuckled and slid back down, poking him in the ribs. "It's a good thing for you, mister."

After a moment of playful poking, Bob laughed and reached over and gave Charlotte a gentle kiss good-night, something he'd done every night since they were married.

"'Night, Char."

"Good night, Bob."

Charlotte closed her eyes, thanking God for the sweet peace that settled upon them. Thoughts of the bed-and-breakfast called to her, luring her away from canning, children and farm life, if only for a moment.

THE NEXT MORNING, the family woke up to smells of fried eggs and sausage still sizzling on the stove. Charlotte pulled hot biscuits out of the oven and gave the sausage gravy a good stir before pouring it into a serving bowl.

"Mm, this smells great," Christopher said, rubbing his stomach as he led the Slater grandkids into the kitchen.

"It sure does," Sam agreed, his hair barely combed.

"Morning, Grandma," was all Emily said, looking as though she'd rather sleep than eat.

The kids had learned well that there was no slacking off on a farm during the summer even though school wasn't in session.

Everyone settled into their seats and Bob said grace over the meal. Plates were passed, but chatter was slow this morning, even though Charlotte could almost always count on Christopher to talk at breakfast. He had barely crept toward his teen years where it seemed the unwritten rule was not to be civil before ten o'clock in the morning.

"I can't believe school starts in a few weeks," Christopher said.

Emily groaned and stabbed her eggs without mercy.

Sam didn't say anything, but Charlotte could see the concern on his face.

"You'll be a big college man," Christopher said, giving his brother a poke on the arm.

Sam shrugged. "No big deal."

Charlotte knew Sam would like to go away to college, but that just wasn't going to work out for their family. It was much more affordable for him to attend Central Community College in Grand Island and commute.

"Well, I'd say it is a big deal. College is nothing to sneeze at, son." The stern tone of their grandpa's voice caused all forks to stop moving while the kids looked at him. "It takes a huge sacrifice on everyone's part, so you are blessed to be able to go."

"It will be a great experience for you, Sam," Charlotte

said gently, hoping to soften Bob's reprimand. She knew Bob's heart and that he meant well, but his voice and expression didn't always reveal his better side.

Sam nodded. "I'm thankful to go, Grandpa," he said, which warmed Charlotte's heart. Many kids would bristle with parental talk like that.

"How's your sewing coming along, Emily?" Charlotte asked, hoping to swing the conversation in a different direction.

Emily shrugged. "I have most of my tops finished. I still need to get some jeans for school." She lifted hopeful eyes to Charlotte.

Charlotte wished she hadn't mentioned it.

"If you want some jeans, you'll need to get a job to pay for them." Bob looked at Emily while chewing a piece of sausage. Bob was happy to provide for the kids and their basic needs, but anything beyond the "basic," well, the kids were expected to help out. He told Charlotte the kids were much too fussy about their clothes, and fussy always meant extra money.

Emily slumped further into her seat.

Charlotte knew Bob was right. Still, she wished he didn't come across so harshly at times. The kids pretty much made their own way and only asked for help when they had no other choice. She knew Emily would find a creative way to get those jeans. Why couldn't Bob see that they were trying?

"Well, there is one thing I'm happy about," Christopher said, his face brightening. "Since I'm going into middle school I'm finally able to join the youth group."

Emily rolled her eyes. Sam gave a grunt.

"What? I think it's cool," he said.

"It is very cool," Charlotte said. "Hard to imagine you're that old already."

"Already?" Christopher looked at her as though she was from another planet. "It's taken me forever to get old enough for people to stop treating me like a baby. I can't wait to hang out with the teenagers."

Charlotte smiled. "I'm glad you feel that way, Christopher. It is a rite of passage, I suppose."

Christopher scrunched his nose. "Rite of what?"

Sam looked at Charlotte. "Just because he's older doesn't mean he's smarter." A smirk played on the corners of his mouth.

Christopher frowned. "Hey, cut it out."

"Just kidding, dude. Don't be so touchy."

"It just means you've reached another phase in your life," Emily said.

"Oh." Christopher toyed with a piece of egg on his plate. "Me and Dylan are looking forward to making new friends."

Charlotte smiled. Dylan Lonetree's family attended the Catholic church in town, but they allowed him to be a part of Christopher's church youth group.

"You'll like it, Christopher," Emily said. "It's a fun group. And Pastor Vink is very cool and creative. I like what he has to say about things, and he plans great activities."

Emily's comments surprised Charlotte. By the look on Bob's face, she'd say they surprised him too.

"Glad somebody is listening to him," Bob said.

"He really is good. I watched him work with the kids at Bible camp, and I can tell he really cares about them."

"Yeah and he was really cool when I worked with him on that project for Shelter for Nebraska," Sam added.

Charlotte watched in amazement as her grandchildren carried on an intelligent, meaningful conversation and held it close to her heart. She knew she'd better. These conversations didn't happen often.

~ Chapter Two

S am and his good friend Jake Perkins sat on the grassy banks of Heather Creek, lazily holding on to their fishing poles and breathing in the fresh country air on a warm Monday afternoon.

Coming from San Diego made Sam a city boy, but he had to admit he enjoyed fishing down at the creek now and then. It didn't really compare to riding the ocean waves, but it involved water and it was relaxing.

"Boy, it feels good to do something besides getting ready to head off for college," Jake said while working a weedy stem between his teeth.

"Dude. You have no idea who's tromped on that or what animal has—"

Jake held up his hand. "Stop right there." He chewed some more and then said, "You'll ruin it for me."

Sam laughed and shook his head. "Your going-away party last week was awesome."

"Yeah. Mom and Dad did a great job planning that one. It was fun to have everyone around and talk about our plans for this coming year." Jake tugged on his pole, wound up the slack in the line, and let it fall back into place. "Sam, you should go away to college, man. It's so lame to stay home."

"I know. But it costs money that I don't have." Sam slapped at an insect on his knee and brushed it off. Did Jake have to remind him that he was being left behind?

"That's why they have scholarships and loans. There's no way I could go away without scholarships." Jake shrugged. "Without scholarships, debt is the name of the game, dude."

Sam shook his head. "Not to Grandpa's way of thinking. I have to—" he used finger gestures to indicate quotes— "'live within my means.'" He rolled his eyes.

"Bummer." A heavy pause fell between them as they seemed to consider Sam's plight.

Jake brightened. "You know, you could spend some weekends with me at the dorm. Once I get settled in I could introduce you to some people around campus. Even if you don't go there you could enjoy some of the campus life." He grinned and gave a wink.

Hope shot through Sam. "Yeah, maybe. Grandma and Grandpa couldn't argue with that since I've saved some money and could afford the gas now and then."

"Great."

Something tugged on Jake's line. He yanked the pole, but whatever it was got away.

"Aw, man."

Sam grinned. "Tough break, dude." He rechecked his pole.

"I have to admit I'm really looking forward to school. I checked out some of the girls while I was on campus, and they were hot." Jake wiggled his eyebrows and lifted a wide grin.

"Cool. Call me naïve, but I think there might be some hot girls at the community college too."

Jake laughed. "Yeah, I guess it could happen. It's gonna be a good year. I can feel it."

"I hope you're right," Sam said.

The buzz of insects flickered through the air while the boys watched their poles. Sam's thoughts tangled like fishing lines. Part of him wanted to go away to college—the larger part of him—and yet, truth be told, he didn't want a lot of debt when he got out of school—especially since he wasn't all that sure what he wanted for his major.

On the other hand, the thought of being out on his own, without his grandparents watching his every move, had definite appeal. He loved his grandparents, but he was tired of being treated like a kid. He was a man now. He wanted to be treated like one. But all Grandpa could talk about was how men also had responsibilities and if he wanted to be treated like a man, he needed to "act" like one.

What about his dad? On second thought, that argument wouldn't work with Grandpa. His dad, after all, hadn't turned out to be all that responsible. How did he get away with that? Sam loved his dad and didn't talk about how he really felt about his absence, but it had taken him a long time to get past hoping his dad would take them home someday. After his dad's visit at Christmas, Sam knew there was no point in hoping any longer. Those days of dreaming were over. Sam would always love his dad, but there would always be a distance between them.

Now that he thought about it, maybe his grandpa was on to something with that responsibility thing.

LATER THAT EVENING, Emily watched as Uncle Bill walked into the kitchen with his wife, Anna, who was carrying their eight-month-old son, Will. Their two young girls, Madison and Jennifer, trailed behind them.

"Glad you were able to come for dinner tonight," Grandma said, mixing dressing into the big chef salad she'd prepared.

Emily was glad her grandma hadn't cooked today because of the summer heat. A nice fresh salad would hit the spot and the dinner rolls in the oven would top the meal off to perfection. Her stomach could hardly bear the wait.

"Worked out well, since Anna and I both had to be in town this afternoon," Uncle Bill said as they settled into their seats.

Grandpa pulled up the high chair for Will and Aunt Anna dipped him into it. Will grinned and babbled to everyone's delight.

"He's growing like a weed," Grandpa said.

Emily studied his chubby legs and arms. She liked that in babies. They looked so soft and huggable.

"Let's pray," Grandpa said.

Once the blessing had been offered, Grandma placed a plate of salad before Emily. "Here you go, honey."

"Thanks, Grandma."

"When you gonna give up that whole vegetarian thing?" Uncle Pete wanted to know.

His wife nudged him in the side.

"It's all right, Aunt Dana. I'm used to his teasing," Emily said. Though Aunt Dana and Uncle Pete had been married for a few months now, Emily still struggled to call the former Miss Simons "Aunt Dana." Maybe one day she'd get used to it.

Aunt Anna grunted and shot Uncle Pete a look.

"Got something stuck in your throat, Anna?" Uncle Pete just wasn't happy unless he was teasing someone. Especially Aunt Anna. Grandma said they mixed like oil and water. Emily didn't know about that, but she could sure tell they were very different from one another.

"Pete, behave yourself," Grandma said.

"You may as well save your breath, Mom. Pete's too old to change now," Uncle Bill said before taking a bite of salad.

Aunt Anna lifted her chin and patted her hair as though to make sure every last strand was in place. Emily considered the likelihood that her aunt actually primped more than she did. And that was saying something.

"You know, Pete, you don't always have to say every little thing that pops into that brain of yours," Aunt Anna said, nose tilted slightly upward.

"On the contrary, dear sister, you can't imagine the restraint I use," Uncle Pete said.

A few snickers made their way around the table before Grandma called a truce and asked who wanted more salad.

"So Dad tells me that Hannah won a trip to the new bed-and-breakfast in Appleton," Uncle Bill said.

Everyone looked at Grandma.

"Yes." Grandma scooped salad into a bowl and passed it around.

"Wow, that's really cool." Emily reached for a dinner roll.

"I never win anything," Sam said glumly.

"Me, neither," said Uncle Pete.

"So are you going to go?" Uncle Bill asked.

"Go where?" Christopher asked, clueless.

All eyes turned to Grandma again. "Hannah won a weekend stay and she's asked me to go with her. Sort of a girls' getaway."

For a moment no one said anything, most likely wondering how this would affect them.

"So are you going to go?" Uncle Bill asked again.

"I don't know. With all the school preparations and such it seems bad timing." Grandma smoothed the napkin on her lap.

"Forget the timing. There will always be something," Uncle Pete said.

"That's what I've been trying to tell her." Grandpa bit a chunk out of his roll.

"It sounds lovely, Charlotte. You really should go," Aunt Anna said.

Aunt Dana agreed.

"See there, it's unanimous," Grandpa said. "You need to go."

Grandma sighed.

"What's the matter, Grandma? Don't you want to go?" Emily couldn't imagine not wanting to go for a girls' getaway weekend. Her grandma hardly ever did anything for herself. Surely, she'd like to get away for some fun now and then.

"I want to go, of course. It's just that there's so much to do."

"We're not babies. It's not like we can't get our things ready for the start of school," Christopher said.

"That's true." Grandma took a sip of her iced tea. "Did you hear that Grandpa is going to work at AA Tractor Supply?"

Emily suspected Grandma was trying to get the conversation off of the getaway weekend.

All eyes turned to Grandpa.

"What's up with that?" Sam asked.

Grandpa grinned. "It's all right for your grandpa to join the ranks of the employed, isn't it?"

"Sure," Uncle Pete said. "Might as well get paid while you're down there yakkin' with the guys."

Grandpa frowned at him, but Uncle Pete just laughed. Then Grandpa explained how he would be filling in for Brad while he went on a trip with his family to Montana to see his wife's relatives.

"That's nice you have the time to help them out," Uncle Bill said.

"Speaking of employment . . . ," Aunt Anna wiped her hands on her napkin and then smoothed it over her lap once again.

"Yes?" Uncle Pete said, feigning interest.

"I was directing this toward Emily," Aunt Anna said dryly.

Emily's head shot up and she looked straight at her aunt.

"Your grandma mentioned you were looking for a little pocket money and we had an idea," Aunt Anna began. "I'd like to hire you to help us out three days a week till school starts. Two of those days, you could help me around the house."

Uncle Pete grunted. Aunt Dana nudged him.

Aunt Anna frowned and then turned back to Emily. "On the third day, I'll go off with the girls for a special day with them, and you'll stay and babysit Will."

Hope bolted through Emily. Maybe she could get those jeans after all. "Yes, yes! I'd love to do it," Emily said.

"I'm so glad to hear that." Aunt Anna picked up her glass of iced tea, took a drink, and then dabbed at her mouth with the napkin before returning it to her lap.

Emily's heart lodged in her throat as she waited to hear the terms of their agreement. Depending on how much they paid her, she might be able to throw in an extra pair of jeans.

"We'll pay you well," Uncle Bill said, as though he knew Emily was mentally sitting on the edge of her seat, waiting for the details.

Aunt Anna smiled.

Quite happy with this turn of events, Emily returned her interest to her plate and pondered the possibilities of the remaining weeks of summer. But before she could mentally fill her wardrobe, Aunt Anna interrupted her thoughts.

"Oh. One more thing. Since Will is so young and you haven't had a lot of experience with children that age, I've taken the liberty of signing you up for a babysitting course that's being offered at Bedford Medical Center starting tomorrow."

Emily sat perfectly still, her mouth gaping like a bass out of Heather Creek.

"You don't have to thank me, dear. We were all too happy to pay for your attendance." Aunt Anna appeared oblivious to the stares coming her way. She took a bite of her salad and then looked back to Emily.

"But here's the real miracle. They only had one opening, and you were the last one to get in." Aunt Anna clapped her hands together and fell back into her seat. "Isn't that wonderful?"

Emily had a word for it all right, but wonderful wasn't it.

Chapter
Three

The next morning Emily walked down the shiny hall at Bedford Medical Center, searching for the room where she would be taking the babysitting course. Hopefully, she could dash into the room before anyone saw her.

Nurses and doctors in white coats padded down the hallway with purpose. The whole thing creeped her out. She had never been a fan of hospitals. They smelled too clean. The white walls were dotted with photos of important doctors and colored arrows.

She turned the corner and spotted the door with the number on it. Taking a deep breath, Emily walked into the room. There were about ten girls already there—most of whom didn't look a day over fourteen.

"Hi, Emily." Up walked Kim Castle. Thirteen-year-old Kim Castle. "What are you doing here?"

"Oh, I thought I'd, um, take the babysitting class."

"Really?" The girl's eyebrows rose, her eyes grew wide. "I would have thought you'd taken it long ago."

"I haven't done much babysitting, really. Seemed like a good idea. Good to see you." Back straight, chin held high, Emily walked across the room and found a seat at the table.

"All right, class, it's time to get started," the teacher said.

While the girls found their seats, the teacher informed them that her name was Nancy Hill and she would be instructing the class. Her voice was strong and confident. She stood tall and important, dressed in a nurse's uniform, padded shoes, and a pleasant smile. She explained that there would be three classes, one this week and two next, each lasting three hours. At the end of the course, they would receive a babysitting certification.

Emily tried to keep her focus on what the instructor was saying, but as she glanced around the room, she could feel her stomach rumble. If ever she had known humiliation, it was now.

At that moment she knew without a doubt that this would be the longest class she would ever take.

LATER THAT AFTERNOON Christopher sat on the porch with his friend, Dylan.

"I'm bored," Christopher said.

"Yeah, me too." Dylan twirled a stick between his fingers. "Maybe your grandma could think of something fun for us to do."

"Are you kidding? If we ask her, she'll give us chores to do. Besides, she's been working in the kitchen for two days canning green beans. She's not in the best of moods." Christopher leaned his jaw into his hand. "Some days it just doesn't pay to get out of bed."

"Yeah." Dylan swatted a fly with his hand. "Hey, I know."

Christopher perked up. "What?"

"We could go bike riding."

"Nah. It's too hot." Christopher sagged again.

"Yeah, I guess."

"We could go to the library."

"I'm not in the mood to read."

"Yeah, me neither."

The boys slumped into silence. The grind of a tractor motor sounded in the distant fields. Toby, the Stevensons' Australian shepherd-blue heeler mix, was a heap of black and brown curled at Christopher's feet.

A car clanked and sputtered as it approached the farm. Pastor Vink's yellow Volkswagen. Toby leapt up and barked a happy welcome to the visitor.

Christopher shook his head. "Our church must not pay Pastor Vink very much. We ought to take up a collection."

Grandma stepped onto the porch, drying her hands on a towel. "Why do you say that?"

"His car makes an awful lot of noise. I think he should lay it to rest."

Grandma chuckled. "My goodness—Old Yeller is his pride and joy. He loves old cars, didn't you know?"

"He does?" Dylan asked.

"Yes. He likes to fix them up now and then. He's had Old Yeller for quite some time now."

"I can tell," Christopher said, watching Old Yeller huff and puff its way up the driveway. "It seems almost as old as—"

Just then Christopher and his grandma locked eyes. The look on his grandma's face was none too friendly. Christopher gulped hard, shoving the remaining unspoken words to a place where they would never see the light of day.

As if choking out its final breath, Old Yeller jerked and hissed once more before belching out a final cough and sputtering to silence. Pastor Vink stepped out and lifted a wide grin. "She ain't what she used to be, but she's still got some life in her," he said.

Christopher never could understand why grown-ups referred to cars as females.

"How are you, Pastor? What brings you out this way?" Grandma asked.

"I was heading out on an errand and thought I'd stop by to see what these guys are up to."

"Oh, okay," Grandma said. "Would you like some iced tea?"

"That would hit the spot for sure," he said. "Mind if I sit down with you boys?"

"Okay." Christopher slid over on the porch swing and Dylan sat on the porch ledge in front of them.

"Sure is a nice day," he said.

"I guess." Christopher's mood hadn't changed all that much.

Dylan drew a circle on the ground with his stick.

"Uh-oh. You've got the summer slumps, huh?"

Christopher and Dylan looked at him and nodded.

"Got any ideas of what we could do?" Christopher asked.

Pastor scratched his jaw. "Hmm, I'll have to think on that a minute. But before I do that, I'd better tell you what I came here to tell you. You know how old people forget things."

Christopher nodded. He wanted to wholeheartedly agree that yes, indeed, he did know how old people forgot things, but one glance at Grandma when she stepped through the front door with a tray of glasses filled with iced tea, and he decided he'd better not risk it.

"This is good, Grandma." He guzzled down half a glass and then swiped his arm across his mouth.

"Glad you like it, Christopher." Grandma turned to Pastor Vink.

"Since I was out this way I wanted to make sure they knew about our upcoming summer workday."

With some reserve, Christopher and Dylan perked up. After all, how fun could a "workday" be? Still, it was a teen event, and these days they qualified.

"The workday will be on Saturday. I have a list of names of some of the elderly in our church who need help with landscaping their homes. Pulling weeds, mowing, raking, that sort of thing."

The more the pastor talked, the more Christopher decided this didn't sound like fun at all. He sometimes helped out his World War II veteran friend, George Kimball, with yard work and it was always exhausting.

"After we finish the work, we're going for a picnic and swim down at Heather Creek."

Now he was talking.

"Awesome," Christopher said. Turning to Dylan, the boys smacked a high five while the grown-ups laughed.

"Looks like you have a couple of workers on your hands, Pastor," Grandma said.

He grinned. "That's good to hear." He drained the last drop of tea from his glass and handed it back to Grandma. "Well, I best be going. I've got to get Old Yeller's oil changed. As long as I maintain her, she serves me well," he said.

Grandma laughed. "Guess the same thing could be said about our tired old bodies." She shot a glance at Christopher to keep him quiet, though he wasn't sure why. He wasn't going to say anything.

"So true. Have a good day, Mrs. Stevenson. Christopher and Dylan, I'll see you at the church on Saturday, nine o'clock sharp." He sauntered down the steps and over to his car. One more wave, and then he climbed inside Old Yeller, which sputtered, coughed, and sneezed all the way down the road until it faded from earshot.

"Well, sounds like you boys are going to have a fun day on Saturday. Get to know the teens a little better too."

Just then Uncle Pete walked up the steps. "Yeah. Better hope they don't have any kind of initiation."

"What?" Something stirred in Christopher's stomach, and he didn't think it was the tea.

"Initiation," Uncle Pete repeated.

Christopher and Dylan exchanged a worried glance. Christopher had heard about such things and he wasn't at all sure he wanted to be involved.

"Oh, you. Stop teasing those boys," Grandma said.

"You mean like they do in college and stuff?" Dylan asked, wide-eyed.

"One and the same." Uncle Pete rubbed his jaw thoughtfully and stared at the sky. "I hope you won't have to eat any spiders. That's the worst."

"Spiders?" the boys said in unison, eyes wide, mouths gaping.

"Peter Charles Stevenson, you stop that this instant."

"Aw, I'm just having a little fun. They know I'm teasing."

Christopher didn't think so. There always seemed to be some hidden meaning behind what grown-ups said. Still, he was pretty sure pastors wouldn't force their church members to eat spiders. It just didn't seem Christian.

Grandma flicked Uncle Pete with her towel and the two of them walked into the house, Uncle Pete laughing with every step.

Dylan turned to Christopher. He looked pale. "Do you think they'll have an initiation?"

"I don't know."

Dylan thought a minute. "I might not be able to come on Saturday. I think I have to clean my room."

"Oh, come on. We'll have to start sooner or later."

Christopher could tell Dylan was rethinking his membership in the youth group.

"We'll be all right. Pastor Vink wouldn't let anyone hurt us."

"You ever heard of pastors gone bad?" Dylan asked.

Christopher and Dylan locked eyes. Suddenly, Christopher thought Saturday might be a good day for him to clean his room too.

SAM CUPPED HIS HAND above his eyes as his gaze swept the sky. Perfect day for flying. They'd had quite a bit of activity today at the Adams County Airport, where he used to work. He missed working there but his uncle Bill's offer of more hours and better pay cleaning and filing at his law firm had been too hard for Sam to resist.

"How you doing, Sam?" Ed Haffner, the manager of the airport, asked.

"Pretty good, I guess." Sam stuffed his hands in his pockets as he watched a plane take off.

"I don't have to tell you we miss you around here," Ed said. "You were a hard worker. How's that new job going?"

"Going pretty well. I keep busy."

Ed nodded. "Busy is good." He smiled. "Oh, by the way, Arielle said to tell you hello the next time I saw you."

"Oh, yeah? How is she doing?"

Arielle had been his girlfriend once upon a time but they had parted ways and he hadn't seen her recently.

"Doing all right, I guess. You know women. Busy, busy."

"Yeah."

"She'll be leaving for school next week. Pretty excited about that, I think."

"Can't blame her there," Sam said, wishing he'd given more thought to the discussions he'd had with her—not that it would have mattered. The outcome would have been the same. He still didn't have the money to go away to school.

"Sure glad you're sticking around so we can see you once in a while. We've got to finish your lessons, you know."

"Yeah." With little money, most of which was going to school payments, Sam didn't think his grandparents would consider flying lessons a high priority.

"You take care, son." He gave Sam a friendly whack on the back and then walked on.

Sam watched a couple more planes descend onto the runway before he climbed into his car and headed for home. The paper on his seat caught his attention. It was the list of textbooks he needed for his classes. He sighed. He couldn't believe the price of textbooks. After going to the college bookstore to buy them, he'd walked away empty-handed, in hopes of finding something on eBay. Even one or two books from eBay would save him money. How did they expect anyone to get a good education?

He didn't know how his friends could afford to go away to school.

Why did life have to cost so much?

AFTER DINNER, Emily and Ashley settled in at Jenny's Creamery for hot fudge sundaes.

"You can't imagine how humiliating it was, Ash. Especially seeing Kim Castle there."

"That had to be awful." Ashley lifted a large scoop of chocolate with her spoon. "At least Kim is nice enough. She's not a blabbermouth, so I doubt she'll go spreading it around."

"Yeah, but she's in junior high. They all like to talk."

"We should know." Ashley laughed.

"I guess."

"Aw, cheer up, Emily. Look at it this way, you only have two more sessions to go."

"Thank goodness."

"What sorts of things did they teach you today anyway?"

She blew out a frustrated sigh. "Good nutrition, first off. Like I don't know about that."

Ashley pointed to Emily's ice cream. "Obviously."

"Hey, whose side are you on anyway?" Emily took a hefty bite of ice cream with chocolate.

Ashley laughed. "Yours." She shrugged. "Sounds like a good place to start. Eat lots of broccoli, all that."

"Whatever. They push veggies, and you know I don't have a problem with that."

"Right. You could probably teach the class." Ashley laughed.

"Well, it would have been less humiliating, that's for sure." They ate a few more bites of ice cream in silence.

"Well, well, well. Fancy meeting you two here."

Emily tensed upon hearing Nicole Evans's voice. She reluctantly looked up into the light blue eyes glaring down at her.

"Hi, Nicole." Her voice sounded icy even to her. She tried not to be that way, but Nicole could be so snotty sometimes.

"Hey, I just ran into Kim Castle," Nicole said with a sparkle in her eye. "She told me she was at a babysitting class today and you were there."

Emily felt her stomach drop with a silent thud. She looked at Ashley, who offered a sympathetic glance.

"Yeah, I was there."

Nicole smirked. "Aren't you kind of old to be taking a

babysitting class? I think I learned about that stuff, oh, I don't know, when I was like, eight."

"I'm sure you don't know everything, Nicole," Ashley defended.

"No, I suppose not. Still, I thought it was funny." She lifted a condescending smile.

A car honked and she turned around. Emily took a deep breath and blew it out.

"Oh, there's Mom. Guess I'll see you around. Have fun at your next *babysitting* class." She waved and headed for her mother's car. Mrs. Evans smiled and waved. Too bad Pastor and Mrs. Evans's kindness hadn't rubbed off on their daughter.

"Sometimes she's nice and sometimes she can be so … so …"

While Ashley searched for the right word, Emily said, "Not nice."

They laughed together. Emily thought it best to forget Nicole for now. "So how is the diner?"

Ashley sighed and shoved her empty ice cream cup aside. "It's there. Seems like ever since camp all I do is work."

"Yeah, but just think of all that extra clothing money you'll have."

"I guess." She ran her fingers through her hair and straightened in her chair. "How are things going with you and Troy?"

"I don't know. Seems like Troy wants to play video games more than he wants to be with me. I haven't even told him the latest about this babysitting adventure."

Ashley shook her head. "Boys are clueless."

Right then a car horn sounded and they turned to see Troy pulling up in his shiny black pickup.

Emily's heart skipped a fast beat. She wasn't sure if it was because she really liked him or because he was the essence of cool.

He got out of his truck, headed inside the ice cream store, and swaggered up to them. "Hey, how's it going?"

"Pretty good," Emily said. She wanted to ask him why he hadn't called in a while, but didn't want him to know she'd noticed.

"Why don't you join us?" Emily asked.

"I'd better get home," Ashley said.

"You don't have to leave." Emily reached for her.

"It's all right. I really do need to get going." Ashley winked. "See you later, Em. Good to see you, Troy."

"Later," Troy said.

"So where you been lately?" he asked.

"Where I've always been. At home."

"Oh." He shoved his hand in his pocket. "What'd you do today?"

Emily told him about the babysitting class.

"It's lame that they would make you do that as old as you are. Kind of funny, though."

Emily frowned. "It's not funny to me."

He reached his hand over and cupped hers. "Sorry. Didn't mean to make you mad."

Every time he did that it sent chills through her. "No problem." She glanced at her watch.

"You need a lift home?"

"Would you mind? Ashley forgot she brought me here."

"Or maybe she didn't and she did me a favor." He winked and they walked back to his truck.

The leather seats squawked beneath them. The scent still smelled new. Troy put the truck into gear and sped off down the road. Emily felt so cool when she was with him.

"I can't believe school starts in a couple of weeks," Troy said over the loud music blaring from his radio.

"Yeah." She didn't feel like yelling. Seemed like if he wanted to talk, he'd turn it down.

"I'm leaving next week to go see my cousin."

Emily turned to him with a start. This was the first she'd heard of it.

"I'll only be staying for a week. Not two weeks like when you went to Bible camp. I'll get back before school starts," he said, ignoring her look of protest.

Never mind that that would leave them very little time together before school started. But she supposed he had the right to go wherever he wanted. They didn't own each other.

"Where does he live?" she asked, trying to ease her frustration—at least in front of him.

"He lives down in southern Nebraska."

"That's nice you get to go," she said.

"Yeah. They live on a lake. It'll be awesome."

She didn't like the look on his face one bit. Lakes meant girls. Great. She'd be stuck babysitting while he was on a beach with other girls.

His truck pulled smoothly up to the drive. "Thanks for the ride," she said, getting out before he could blink. She slammed the door and walked to the house without a backward glance.

Emily had barely stepped into the house when the phone rang. It was probably Ashley wondering how the ride home was. She was so mad at Troy, she wasn't sure she could even talk to Ashley about it right now.

"Emily, phone call for you. It's Mrs. Hill, your babysitting instructor." Grandma had a question on her face.

"Don't know why she'd be calling me," Emily muttered, walking to the phone.

"Hello?"

"Emily, this is Mrs. Hill. I wanted to talk to you about helping me out in the class next week. You're a little older than the other girls, and it's quite obvious you know what you're doing when it comes to children, so I'd like you to be my aide next week. Would you be willing to do that?"

"Uh, well, sure."

"No surprises. I'll just have you help me demonstrate some techniques, pass out papers and pencils, that sort of thing. You game?"

"Yeah."

"Thanks. I knew I could count on you."

Emily hung up the phone and explained to Grandma what the call was about.

Grandma raised her eyebrows. "Well, that says something that she would call you for that." She looked impressed.

Emily wasn't. She was the only one over fourteen.

Chapter Four

With the morning sun warming her back, Emily shut the door of her grandma's car, tucked the keys into her handbag and strode up the sidewalk to Uncle Bill and Aunt Anna's home. The light scent of roses lifted from the bushes that bordered the front of the house.

"Good morning, Emily." The front door swung open and Aunt Anna stood there in a beautiful mint-green outfit of capri pants and matching top, her hair, grin, and makeup perfectly in place. Emily couldn't imagine Aunt Anna ever living on a farm. "So good of you to start your day with us this morning. Come on inside."

Start her day? Should she mention she'd already collected eggs from the chicken coop?

Emily got a whiff of Aunt Anna's heavy perfume when she brushed past her and stepped inside. Emily didn't even know people wore perfume this early in the morning.

Once inside, she glanced around. No matter how many times she'd seen this house, Emily could never get used to how it always sparkled, despite three children living there. Something told Emily she would earn every penny she made from working at Uncle Bill and Aunt Anna's house.

Her gaze swept through the hallway and over to the dining room. The ceramic tile in the hallway didn't have a speck of dirt on it anywhere. Aunt Anna caught her staring at the floor.

"Oh, good, you noticed. The grout between those tiles is filthy. I thought it would be a good place for you to start this morning."

Emily looked at the line of grout between the tiles and couldn't see any dirt. She had a feeling this was going to be a very long day.

Madison and Jennifer ran into the hallway and skidded to a halt in front of her.

"Remember, girls, ladies never run in the house."

"Yes, Mommy," the girls said in unison.

"Hi, Emily," Madison said with a large grin on her face. "I'm excited you're here."

"Me too," Jennifer piped up.

"I want to show you my American Girl doll," Madison said. "I can read one of the books to you too."

"I have new shorts on." Jennifer smiled and twirled to give Emily the full effect.

Emily laughed.

"All right, girls, that's quite enough. You need to give Emily some breathing room. Besides, Mommy needs to show her some things first. You go play quietly in your rooms, and then we'll come see you in a little while."

"Okay, Mommy."

Both girls reached over and gave their mother a hug and skipped their way back to their rooms.

Aunt Anna smiled and shook her head. "They are full of energy."

"Where's Will?" Emily asked.

"Oh, he's taking a nap. He'll be up soon. Walk with me to the utility room. We'll get our cleaning supplies in there."

Before long, Aunt Anna had Emily kneeling on the ceramic tile in the entryway, scrubbing the grout with a toothbrush.

"That should keep you busy for a while. In the meantime, I think I'd better go check on the baby." Aunt Anna turned and headed down the hallway.

Digging into the grout with the toothbrush, Emily started to wonder if those jeans were going to be worth all the effort.

"KNOCK, KNOCK," Hannah called from the back door of the Stevensons' house.

"Come on in, Hannah." Charlotte swept the last crumb off the floor and into the dustpan. When she stood, she brushed back a strand of hair from her face and let out a groan.

"Wow, you've been busy," Hannah said, admiring the rows of recently canned green beans and tomatoes.

"I sure have." Though Charlotte was more tired than she could say, she had to admit she loved the feeling of accomplishment when she finished canning so many vegetables. The house smelled of cooked vegetables, and the neat rows of jars on her counter, filled to the brim with beans and tomatoes, were a sight to behold.

Hannah turned to her. "Oh, you don't look so good."

"Thanks a lot."

Hannah chuckled. "I'm sorry. I mean, you look tired."

"I just finished three days of canning vegetables. I am tired. Tea?"

"Of course." Hannah walked over and grabbed the mugs from the cupboard and helped Charlotte get their drinks ready—tea for Hannah, coffee for Charlotte.

They slid into their wooden chairs at the table.

"I'm thankful for the break this morning." Charlotte took a sip from her mug while Hannah eyed her suspiciously. "What?"

"You had a checkup lately?"

"What kind of checkup?"

"You know, just a general checkup to make sure everything is running the way it should."

This time Charlotte chuckled. "Hannah. You saw all the canning I've had to do this week. That would make anyone tired."

"That's true. Still, I think you need that checkup."

Charlotte sighed, thinking it truly was time for a checkup, though she hated to take the time. But she hadn't been sleeping well, so she needed to check into that. Too much on her mind, most likely, thinking about what she needed to get done before the kids started back to school.

"I know you're right. I'll check into it. There's just so much to do—it's hard to take the time."

"Charlotte, you have to make time for yourself. If you don't take care of you, who will?"

"I suppose." Charlotte sighed and stared into her coffee cup, allowing the strong brew to fill her senses.

"That's why you need this girlfriend weekend."

Charlotte looked up and smiled. "It does sound wonderful."

"Please, Charlotte, you just have to go."

"That's what Bob said."

"He did? See there. I know he's always looking out for you. You're awfully tired. The time away would do you good. Then you would be more refreshed and ready to help everyone through their first few weeks of school." Hannah cradled the mug between her hands, eyes full of pleading.

"I suppose."

"It's a beautiful setting. We can leisurely stroll from shop to shop, relaxing over a cup of coffee. No alarm clocks."

Charlotte let out a contented sigh. "Heavenly."

"Then you'll go?" Hannah asked, hopeful.

Charlotte bit her lip and then let out a sigh. "I guess I will."

"Well, don't act so happy about it," Hannah said, a bit irritated.

"I'm sorry, Hannah," Charlotte said. "I really am honored that you would choose me to go with you."

"Yeah, it shows," Hannah said with obvious sarcasm.

"What are you honored about?" Bob asked when he walked into the kitchen and grabbed himself a cup of coffee.

"I just told Hannah I would go to the bed-and-breakfast with her."

"Good for you." Filling his mug, Bob walked to the table. "Okay if I join you ladies?"

"Sure, sit down," Hannah said.

"Smells good in here," he said, looking at the counter. "You've been busy."

"Yes, I have. What's on your agenda today?" Charlotte asked.

"I'm headed over to the tractor supply to start my job."
He smiled.

"Your job? Am I missing something?" Hannah asked.

Bob explained how he would be filling in, helping Andy
Weber while Brad was on vacation.

"Well, that sounds like a good deal. Frank will look forward to jawing with you when he goes over for coffee."

"He jaws with me every day. Only this time I'll be working, so I may not have as much fun," Bob said.

"Oh, yeah, I'm sure Andy is a harsh taskmaster," Charlotte
said with a chuckle. She couldn't imagine anyone as old
and frail as Andy being harsh about anything.

"Well, anyway, I hope I'll be a help to them." He yawned.
"Plus, it will give me something to do."

Charlotte studied him. Retirement wasn't coming easily
for Bob. He had just finished helping Pete with a lot of the
spring planting and would no doubt be helping again with
the harvest. Still, he was trying to let Pete do the majority
of the work. Bob wasn't the type to sit around and do nothing. This job seemed to give him a sense of well-being.
Maybe she would suggest later that he look for a part-time
job. It could be just what he needed.

"Where are the kids?" Hannah asked.

"Sam's working at Bill's firm today. Christopher is over
at Dylan's and Emily is working for Anna."

"Bill's Anna?"

"That very one."

The timer on the pressure cooker rattled and hissed from
the stove.

"Oh, she'll earn every penny," Hannah said.

They all shared a laugh.

"She certainly will," Charlotte finally said. "She will also get to know Anna on a whole new level."

Just then Toby whined at Charlotte's feet.

"What's the matter with you?"

Toby got up and walked over to the door.

"Oh, all right." Charlotte rose from her chair and let her outside. "Seems I'm at everyone's beck and call—even the dog's."

Hannah laughed.

"Uh-oh. I think that's my cue to go. You ladies behave yourselves." Bob finished the last of his coffee, rinsed the mug in the sink, and headed out the door. "I'll be home in time for dinner," he called out.

"Well, I'll let you go so you can finish your chores. I've got a few chores of my own to take care of." Hannah rinsed out her cup.

"Hannah? Thanks again for asking me."

"Just try to show a little enthusiasm, even if you do have a million other things to do."

"Okay."

Charlotte saw her to the door. "Do you know what I think?"

"What?"

"I think you missed your calling."

Hannah's eyebrows lifted. "Yeah?"

"Yeah. You should have been a salesman."

JUST BEFORE DINNERTIME, Charlotte worked in the vegetable garden. More green beans. Oh, she could manage her own green beans, all right, but after getting all those green beans from her neighbor, who couldn't use any more, she just didn't know how she could do it all. She had never canned so many jars in one summer in all her life. And by the looks of the summer's bounty, she still had plenty more to put up.

A fly buzzed near her ear and she swatted it away, nearly toppling the straw hat from her head. The sun beat down on her as she plucked the ripe beans from the vines. She had meant to get this done this morning, but with everything else she had to do, she hadn't gotten around to it.

The vines drooped with beans. She had no idea so many beans were ready. With a sigh, she scooted along the row, her plastic bag beneath her, bucket in her hand, while she continued to throw in the beans.

She had hoped to work in the flower garden today too, but the sun's rays were relentless. It would have to wait until the cool of the evening or tomorrow. No, she couldn't do it tomorrow. She had to work early at the Bedford Gardens Convalescent Center. Oh, well, she would have to take things one day at a time.

With a grunt, she heaved herself off the ground and brushed the dirt from her gloves and legs. Grabbing her bucket of beans, she headed for the house. She'd have to work on the farm books this afternoon too. She couldn't remember if there were any bills due. Every joint in her body hurt. All Charlotte wanted to do was take a nap.

Once inside the house, she spotted the phone book. Browsing through it, she picked up the phone. Hannah was right. It wouldn't hurt for her to have a checkup with Dr. Carr. Maybe he could give her a vitamin that would put a little pep in her day. She knew people who swore by vitamins. One thing was for sure: she needed something.

Once she had made her appointment and hung up the phone, she turned to see Emily standing in the kitchen.

"Oh, I didn't hear you come in." One glance at her granddaughter made Charlotte wonder just how hard Anna had worked her today.

"Are you sick?" Emily asked.

"What?"

"Are you sick?" Emily asked again, worry lining her face.

It suddenly registered that Emily had overheard her conversation with the nurse.

"Oh, no, honey, I'm fine. Just a little tired. Thought it was time for my annual checkup."

Emily eyed her warily. "You would tell me, right? I mean, if there were something wrong?"

"There's nothing wrong. Yes, I would tell you." Charlotte walked over and grabbed some iced tea from the refrigerator. "Now, tell me about your day."

"Nothing to tell, really. I cleaned all day." Emily practically dropped into her chair.

Living on a farm, Charlotte knew that Emily was no stranger to work. She had plenty of chores around here. So whatever Anna assigned to her had definitely taken its toll.

"Did you know people have to clean the grout between ceramic tiles? I used a toothbrush on it. Have you ever noticed how many tiles are in their entryway?" Emily shoved her chin into her palm. "I'll never look at it the same."

Charlotte tried to hide her amusement. No doubt this would be a good experience for Emily. She only hoped she wouldn't hold it against Anna when the work was all over.

"Just keep those jeans in sight," Charlotte encouraged.

"What jeans?" Emily grinned.

Charlotte walked over to the refrigerator and pulled out a package of chicken. The back door swung open and in walked Bob, looking every bit as haggard as Emily.

"You all right?"

"I'm fine," he said. "Let me know when dinner is ready. I'm going to my chair." With that he stomped off, leaving Charlotte and Emily scratching their heads.

"Hey, Emily, you going to help out with teen workday this Saturday?" Christopher asked when he walked into the kitchen.

"Oh, don't mention work," she said, grabbing her head.

"What's wrong with her?" he asked Charlotte.

She smiled. "It's been a long day. She worked for Aunt Anna."

Christopher's eyes grew wide. "Oh."

No further explanation was needed.

"Are you getting excited about the workday, Christopher?" Charlotte asked, dipping the chicken in a cornflake batter coating before placing it in the frying pan.

"Well, I'm looking forward to hanging out with the teens and swimming at the creek, if that's what you mean."

Charlotte tossed him a look. "Won't hurt you to help some people along the way."

"Yeah, I guess." He walked over to the stove. "What's for dinner?"

"Fried chicken, mashed potatoes, green beans, corn on the cob, applesauce. How does that sound?"

He looked at his belly and rubbed it. "Did you hear that?" He lifted a heart-melting grin. "It sounds great."

Charlotte laughed and gave him a sideways hug.

"Go get washed up and you can help me set the table tonight. Give your sister a break." She winked at Emily.

Emily smiled. "Thanks, Grandma. I'm going to my room for a minute and then I'll be back down."

Charlotte watched Emily trudge out of the kitchen and wondered if she would ever get those jeans.

⌣ Chapter Five

Finishing up his work at the law office, Sam lifted a few more legal documents from the filing tray and shoved them into the appropriate files. Fresh coffee filled the carafes even though it was past five o'clock. He knew that Uncle Bill and his partner Donald Simpson would be at work for a couple more hours yet. Sam couldn't imagine what the pull was for people to get into law. They rifled through paperwork all day and worked late hours. No amount of money could make him do that. He wanted a career that would take him places, not put him behind a desk for fifty years, cracking open old law books and reading about boring disputes between people. No, his life would be different from Uncle Bill's. He shoved the last of the filing away. Unfortunately, he first had to get through college.

When Sam got home, he had a few minutes to spare before dinner. He scanned his e-mail first, and spotted a note from his friend Jordan in San Diego.

Hey, Sam. Just checking in and seeing how things are going for you. We've had some awesome surfing weather here. You'd love it.

Sam wondered if he'd even remember how to surf now.

Anyway, the guys and I were wondering if you could come out here for a few days before school starts. If money is an issue, my dad would probably be happy to send you the money just so I'd quit nagging him about it.

Sam grinned. He was glad Jordan wanted him there, but he couldn't accept money from his dad for that. There was a time when he might have done that but not anymore. He wondered if that meant he was growing up after all.

Well, think about it, buddy. It sure would be fun to get the group together again for a day of surfing. Just let me know. Jordan.

Great. One more thing to make him wish he wasn't going to college in a week.

"Sam, it's time to eat," Grandma called out.

Sam clicked out of his e-mail and went into the kitchen where the rest of the family had gathered. The fried chicken and vegetables looked delicious. He was hungry. He tried not to think about the idea that he might know that chicken. Such was farm life—or so his uncle Pete told him.

After Grandpa said grace, they dug into the meal.

"How was your day, Emily?" Grandpa asked.

She shrugged. "Okay."

"Just okay?" he pressed.

"I worked for Aunt Anna." Emily told them how she scrubbed grout all morning.

"Get you in good training for when you get married," Sam said.

"Who said I'll be the one doing the housework? Maybe my husband will do it," Emily snapped.

Sam figured he'd get a rise out of her. He pitied her future husband. He could suggest she do the filing where he worked, but he might start a feud, so he opted against it.

"Things busy at the office today, Sam?" Grandma asked.

"Like always. Endless paperwork."

Grandma chuckled. "I know all about that. The paperwork around here alone gives me a headache."

"See, school isn't the only place where you have to work," Grandpa said.

Head down, Sam stirred the food on his plate. He hoped Grandpa wasn't gearing up for another lecture. "Yeah, I guess," he mumbled.

"I don't know why everyone is so glum." Christopher took a bite of chicken. "I had a great day."

"That's because you're a kid," Sam said.

"What's that got to do with it?" Christopher wanted to know.

"You don't have any real responsibilities yet. You can do what you want." Sam wished he could go up to his room. He didn't really want to talk to everyone tonight.

"No, I can't. Grandma and Grandpa don't let me do whatever I want."

Emily rolled her eyes.

"Forget it," Sam said. He scooped the last bite of meat from his plate. "Can I be excused?"

"May I?" Grandma corrected.

Sam blew out a sigh. "May I?"

"Yes. If you don't want any blueberry pie."

"I don't want any." With that he shifted his chair back.

"Can I have his piece?" Christopher asked.

Sam imagined Grandma made a face at Christopher but he didn't see. He walked to the sink, rinsed off his plate, and then walked out of the kitchen without another word.

They were, no doubt, watching him and wondering what was wrong. His favorite pie was blueberry. But he just didn't have it in him to talk tonight.

He had lots of thinking to do.

AFTER DINNER, Emily spotted her grandma bent over in the flower garden. She went outside.

"Need some help?"

Grandma stood up and grabbed her back with a groan. "Guess I'm not as young as I used to be." She threw the weeds she was holding into a nearby pile.

"I can finish weeding, Grandma. Why don't you go in and rest? You've been working really hard lately."

Grandma stared at her so long, Emily felt her face flush. "What?"

"You don't want anything, do you? Last time you cleaned the house, it was so I'd let you go to Bible camp," Charlotte teased.

"No, Grandma. You just seem tired and I wanted to help. No ulterior motives, I promise," Emily said with a smile.

They laughed together.

"That's very thoughtful, Emily. I just need that last row weeded, dear, if you can manage."

"I can manage."

"Then I think I will go in and sit down."

Emily nodded and set to work. When her grandma's back was turned, Emily watched her walk toward the house. She seemed a little slower than usual.

Please, God, don't let anything be wrong with Grandma.

Under the canopy of a dusky sky, Emily pulled weeds while her thoughts turned to one day getting a decent job and saving money for a car. She had finally gotten her license, but she could only drive occasionally, using her grandma's car. Most of her friends had cars of their own. She felt like such a baby.

She pulled out the root of a long weed with a vengeance. Seemed like weeds could grow up overnight. She sure wished she could do that.

Her friends couldn't believe she'd actually had to take a babysitting course just to watch Will. Did Aunt Anna think she was that irresponsible? How hard could it be to watch a baby?

Emily tugged and pulled on roots, loosening the dirt around them. A worm squirmed in the soil when she disturbed his place. Emily grimaced. If there was one thing she didn't like, it was bugs and worms and such. Probably because Sam used to chase her with them when they were kids. She'd better not show him this one or he might revert to the old days.

"Emily, you're wanted on the telephone," her grandmother called out.

"Be there in a minute." She pulled the last weed from the flower garden and tossed it into the pile. She'd come back out and put the weeds in the compost pile after she answered the phone.

Brushing the dirt from her hands and stomping the

bottoms of her sandals on the back stoop, she entered the kitchen.

"It's Troy," Grandma mouthed, before leaving the room, giving her privacy.

"Thanks." Emily grabbed the phone. "Hey, Troy."

"How's my best girl?"

A slight shiver shot right through her. "I'll bet you say that to all the girls." He most likely did say that to his former girlfriends, but for now, she'd revel in it.

"Aw."

That was all he said.

"I'm good." She told him how she'd been weeding in the flower garden.

"Hey, there's a good movie coming out on Friday night in Harding. I thought since I'll be leaving next week, maybe we could go to the movie together before I go?"

"Sure. Wait. I'd better check with Grandma first. Can you call me back in about half an hour and I can let you know then?"

"Can't you ask her now?"

"Timing is everything," she said.

"Yeah, I guess." He sounded annoyed. "Why do you always have to ask for every little thing?"

"Don't you?"

"No. My mom trusts me."

"Well, I think my grandparents trust me. They just want to know what's going on." She hadn't really minded much in the past, but lately Troy had been pressuring her with his questions.

"Whatever. Sometimes I just think—oh, never mind."

"No, go ahead. What do you think?" She wasn't sure she wanted to hear, but, on the other hand, she had to know.

"Okay, but remember, you asked for it. Sometimes I think they treat you like a baby. I mean, they didn't let you go to prom, and I tried to understand that, but a movie? I don't get it."

The words went through her ears and churned in her stomach.

"I'm sorry," he continued. "But that whole thing with the babysitting class and stuff like that. It seems a little weird."

"Well, that was my aunt Anna, not my grandparents."

"Yeah, but they agreed to it. They could have rescued you and said you didn't need to do that. They trusted that you could handle it, that sort of thing."

"I guess." He was putting her in a bad mood.

"Well, I'll call back in half an hour. See if you can go to the movie at seven, then out to eat."

"Okay."

"Talk to you soon." He hung up.

She could tell Troy's patience was wearing thin with her. If her grandparents didn't stop being so overprotective, he'd dump her. She didn't want him to dump her. Why couldn't they let her grow up?

Emily went to the bathroom and by the time she came back to the kitchen, she spotted Grandma sitting at the table, sipping iced tea. That was good. She was usually calm and relaxed when she did that.

"Okay if I join you for a few minutes before I put the weeds on the compost pile?"

"Sure. Help yourself," Grandma said. "You didn't talk to Troy very long."

"No." She washed her hands, dropped ice cubes into her glass causing a clunk or two, and then poured the tea over it, making the ice crackle and pop. She slid into her chair. "He wanted to know if I could go to a movie on Friday night with him."

"Oh, I see. Which movie is it?"

"I don't know. I didn't ask."

"Well, you know the rules, Emily. You can't go to just any movie. It has to be approved by your grandpa and me."

The pressure increased. If she asked Troy what they were going to see, it would just prove his point that she had to go to them with every little thing. "If it's a decent movie, can I go?"

Grandma thought a moment. "I think that would be all right."

"He thought we could go to a movie, then out to eat afterward." Emily took a drink from her tea.

"As long as you're back home by eleven, that would be fine, I think."

Emily relaxed a little. But she still had to find out what movie. She loved her grandparents, but she was beginning to see why her mother had found it hard to live with their rules. Emily definitely looked forward to getting out on her own one day.

Chapter Six

By the next afternoon, Charlotte had most things in order around the house so she could go to Bedford Gardens Convalescent Center with a clear conscience. No matter how tired she was, her visits there always perked up her spirits considerably.

The renovations at the center continued, though at a snail's pace. They had to do a little here and there as money allowed. Heading up the sidewalk to the center, Charlotte noticed the weeds muddling the flowerbed. Their groundskeeper had been on sick leave. Obviously, they hadn't assigned someone to do his work lately. She'd take care of it herself if she had the strength. Maybe she'd mention the matter to Pastor Vink for their teen workday—if not this Saturday, they might fit it in another day.

No wheelchairs lined the front of the building today. Much too warm outside. Children played in the neighborhood, running and riding bikes, unaffected by the weather.

Across the street, two toddlers splashed and squealed in a kiddie pool while their mothers looked on.

Charlotte pulled open the entrance door and stepped inside, thankful to be out of the heat. Pulling a handkerchief from her pocketbook, she patted her face dry.

"It's a scorcher out there today," a bright-faced young woman with long brown hair and a pleasant smile said.

Charlotte nodded and walked over to the receptionist's desk. "I'm Charlotte Stevenson," she said, extending her hand. "You must be new here?"

"Yes, I'm Amber Walker. Just started yesterday," she said with an air of pride.

"Good to have you on board. I volunteer my time here a few hours a week."

Her eyes sparkled. "That's great. It's such a rewarding job, I'm sure. My grandma lives in a nursing home in another state, and I sure wish I could be there. But I'm thankful for the people who encourage her when I can't."

Charlotte smiled. How refreshing to meet a young woman who truly had a heart for the elderly.

"Well, I'm going to head over to the Alzheimer's ward. Nice to meet you."

"You, too," Amber said.

Charlotte continued on down the hall, waving at the workers and patients along the way. She popped in to Bertha Webber's room first. Bertha was a lifetime resident of Bedford and a former schoolteacher. Although she was in the beginning stages of Alzheimer's she usually recognized familiar faces.

"How are you today, Bertha?"

"Who is it?" Bertha asked. She squinted her eyes and took a moment to focus.

"It's Charlotte Stevenson."

"Well, why didn't you say so? Charlotte, get yourself on in here." Bertha straightened the shawl around her and patted her hair. "I must look an awful sight." She raised a gnarled finger. "Now, don't you go back and tell everyone what a mess I'm in. I just wanted to be a little lazy today."

Charlotte chuckled. "Your secret is safe with me." She bent down and kissed the old woman's soft but wrinkled forehead. "Besides, you look just fine."

"Tell me what those kids are up to these days."

She asked Charlotte that same question every time she came to visit. Bertha had a heart for children, young and old.

"They're getting ready to start another year of school."

Bertha clucked her tongue. "My, my, where does the time go?"

"Sam's starting college this year."

"You don't mean it. Sam in college. Why, they're growing up before our eyes, Charlotte."

"That they are. Emily's driving now."

She clutched her chest. "Heavens to Betsy. Good thing I'm staying off the streets." She cackled.

Charlotte laughed with her. "She does all right. Truth be told, I'd rather ride with her than Sam."

"Oh, yes, boys get a little heavy on that gas pedal, don't they?"

"Too much adrenaline shooting through them down to their toes, I suppose," Charlotte said, walking over to a bouquet of flowers on a table. "These are lovely." She took a long whiff, and then adjusted a stem or two.

"From my neighbor, Irene Grammon. Good friend." With a groan Bertha rearranged herself on the chair. "Yeah, the old gray mare just ain't what she used to be."

Charlotte laughed. "You're not a mare."

"Well, thanks for the vote of confidence." Bertha studied Charlotte a moment. "You sick?"

Charlotte looked at her. "No, why do you ask?"

"You got dark circles under your eyes. Aren't you sleeping at night?"

First, she can't see me and now she sees dark circles. "I do all right."

"Don't kid a kidder. You're worried over something or not getting your rest."

"No, I'm fine, really. Just got some things on my mind, getting the kids ready for school, all that. Not much to do, though, so I don't know why I'm fussin' about it." Charlotte smiled.

"Well, you'd better take care of yourself or you'll end up like me."

"Thanks for the tip. I'd better go visit some other folks too. You stay out of trouble."

"I'll do my best."

Charlotte gave her friend a gentle hug, and then walked out of the room. Making her way down the hall, her fingers absently patted beneath her eyes.

ON CHARLOTTE'S WAY HOME from Bedford Gardens, she decided to stop by AA Tractor Supply to check on Bob. After all, she hadn't seen him at work in his new position yet.

Once in the parking lot, she climbed out of the car and walked toward the store entrance. A smattering of customers' cars lined the lot. She wondered if they were paying customers or farmers coming in to shoot the breeze.

The door jangled when she entered. The room smelled of home improvement products and cleaning supplies—a scent that always made her want to go home and start fixing up her nest.

Though she spotted a few customers, she didn't see Andy or Bob anywhere, but she heard Andy's voice, faint at first and then stronger.

"Then put those boxes over in that room. You'll need to rearrange the product on the shelf. Oh, and call Dan Morris and let him know his part came in today. Better get out in the storefront. There are a few customers waiting. Then come back and I'll give you some more instructions on that order."

Charlotte heard a frustrated sigh, followed by heavy boots tromping across the wooden floor.

"May I help you?" she heard Bob say.

The customer referred to an item she couldn't find and Charlotte peeked around a can of dust spray to get a glimpse of Bob. His face was pinched and serious.

Once he and the customer walked to the opposite side of the store, Charlotte's footsteps creaked quietly across the floor and she slipped out of the store. Better not let him suspect she had overheard anything.

Before she could get in the car, her thoughts were already whipping up dinner, complete with apple caramel pie, Bob's favorite. She had an idea that tonight he might need it.

Looked like the next few weeks just might be a lot longer than Bob had planned.

FRIDAY NIGHT didn't come soon enough for Emily. She put the finishing touches on her outfit and fussed with her hair one more time. A radio blared an indiscernible tune and tires crunched pebbles in the driveway. She peeked out her window.

Troy.

Her heart gave a flutter and she went back to the dresser. With one more swipe of lip gloss, she rubbed a smudge from beneath her eye and waited a moment till she heard him come in the door. She never wanted to appear too anxious.

"Troy, good to see you. Come on in," Emily heard her grandmother say.

"What are you all dressed up for?" Christopher asked him.

Emily rolled her eyes. She'd better get downstairs and rescue him from her little brother. When she stepped on the first stair, it creaked and Troy looked up.

"Hey, Emily."

"Hi." Her face grew warm. She hoped it didn't show.

"You'd better come in and say goodbye to your grandpa before you go," Grandma suggested.

Emily cringed inside. Why did they have to go through such a ritual just to get out the door? No other girl she knew had to go through this. It was so embarrassing. What must Troy think of her and her family?

"Grandpa, we're getting ready to leave for the movie," Emily said.

He looked up from his newspaper.

"All right." He looked at Troy and gave a curt nod. "You have her back home by eleven, young man."

"Yes, sir."

Could she possibly be any more humiliated? Did they think they still lived in the days of Ward and June Cleaver? Her grandpa watched way too many old movies. She wanted to die on the spot.

They said goodbye to her grandma and then walked outside to Troy's truck. At least they didn't ask her what movie they were going to. She didn't know. Right now, she couldn't deal with one more question.

Troy opened the door for her.

"Thanks." She slipped onto the leather seat.

Troy walked around to the driver's side and climbed inside. "Boy, they sure are strict, aren't they?"

"Yeah." Emily figured he'd dump her soon. He could have any girl at school, so why would he bother with her when her grandparents were so strict?

He eased out of the driveway. No doubt, he saw Grandma looking out the window at them too. Emily felt like a kindergarten student on her first day of school. It wasn't as though this was her first date. But each date was the same. They watched after her like a child. When would they look at her as an adult?

"You look good tonight."

Her stomach flipped. "Thanks." She wondered what she had been thinking at camp when she'd had a small crush on that boy Mike. She was lucky to have Troy.

"I'm glad you could come tonight."

"Me too." She hoped he wouldn't meet someone else when he went to visit his cousin. She'd have to make sure he'd miss her while he was away.

Chapter Seven

Charlotte sat in her rocking chair while Bob watched an old Ma & Pa Kettle movie on television. She had hoped to finish the embroidery on this pillowcase by now, but she hadn't found the time.

Bob looked over at her. "Where did you say the kids were tonight?"

"Sam went over to Jake's house, Emily went to the movies with Troy, as you know, and Christopher is upstairs with Dylan who is spending the night before their big teen outing tomorrow." She smiled.

"Oh, that's right. I don't know what Emily sees in that boy with his fancy truck."

"Now who's struggling to let go?" she teased.

Bob shrugged. "Maybe."

Charlotte smiled and worked the thread through the soft linen between her fingers. When Denise lived at home, she had been "Daddy's Girl." Now, it appeared, Emily had morphed into "Grandpa's Girl." Charlotte's heart melted with the thought.

Bob might be a little crusty around the edges when it came to discipline and the serious side of life, but deep down, she knew he had the heart of a marshmallow. He just kept it very well hidden.

"I just want her to make sure she likes the boy for more than just his fancy truck," he said.

"I don't think that's it, Bob. Emily's not that superficial."

Bob looked at her. "Aren't most girls that age superficial?"

Charlotte thought about that. "Well, you'd better never let her hear you say that. Besides, that's a pretty broad sweep, don't you think?"

"Maybe. Seems like all they do is sit around and giggle."

"Now, Bob Stevenson, you know that's not true. Emily works hard around here. Now she's working for Bill and Anna too. In fact, I think she's quite responsible for a girl her age."

"Aw, I know it. I'm just saying, I hope she looks for character in a young man, rather than a nice vehicle. That's all I'm saying."

"She's not picking a husband just yet."

"You never know."

Charlotte chuckled. "You're a worrywart." She thought it amusing that their conversations were usually the other way around. She was the worrier and he always told her to let go and trust. But tonight, Grandpa's Girl was out in a truck with a young man. That evidently changed things.

Just then the phone rang. "I'll get it." Charlotte laid aside her embroidery and walked over to the phone. "Hello?"

"Charlotte. This is Allison Cunningham."

"Yes, Allison. How are you?"

"Oh, I'm fine. But I thought I should tell you something."

Charlotte rolled her eyes and took a deep breath. She never knew what Allison might say next, but the woman had a penchant for gossip with a side of meanness. "Oh?"

"Well, I thought you would like to know that I am on my way to Hannah's to work on a project for the hospitality group and I just passed Emily and some boy standing by a black truck at the side of the road."

Charlotte gasped. "Were they all right?"

"They were totally fine, as far as I could tell," Allison said as though implying something else.

"Well, they must have had a problem. I'd better check on her."

"I'm sure they're fine. You know how kids are. Probably talking . . . or *something*."

Charlotte could feel her blood pressure rise. "Thank you for letting us know, Allison."

"You're welcome. I'm surprised Hannah didn't ask you to join us to work on plans for the church picnic. It would have been nice to see you."

"Uh, yeah. Well, I've got a lot on my plate at the moment. Thanks again. Talk to you soon." Charlotte hung up before she could give that woman a piece of her mind. Charlotte would never understand why Allison always wanted to make others feel bad.

"What was that about?" Bob wanted to know.

"Oh, it was Allison Cunningham. You know how she loves to stir up trouble."

He chuckled and shook his head. "What's she up to this time?"

"I'll tell you in a minute. I need to make a phone call first." Charlotte went into the other room to call Emily on her cell phone. No need to get Bob upset.

Emily's cell phone went to voice mail, and Charlotte could only offer up a prayer that her granddaughter was alright. She headed back into the family room where Bob was asleep in his chair. She settled into her own chair and tried to distract herself with a silly TV show, but it was hard not to be worried about Emily. On top of that, she couldn't help wondering what Hannah and Allison were doing right now.

"DUDE, WHERE ARE YOU getting all your money for school clothes?" Sam asked when he and Jake exited a store at the mall in Harding, a bulging bag in Jake's hand.

Jake grinned. "You ever hear of credit cards?"

Smells of perfume, hot pretzels, and cookies mingled together and then filled the hallways. Sam took a deep breath.

"Oh." His shoes scuffed the cement floors as they headed for the next store. He didn't have any credit cards. He knew how his grandpa felt about debt, but right now he could use a little extra credit. His buddies were all going away to school while he was stuck on a farm, it just wasn't fair. The least he could do was enjoy a little materialism along the way.

"How hard is it to get a Visa, do you know?" Sam asked.

"Are you kidding? They make it so easy for everyone that it is ridiculous. Of course, they don't care how far in debt you get." Jake shrugged. "I try to pay it off as soon as I can."

Sam nodded. He would do that too. He had a good job at the law office. Still, he had school bills, car upkeep and insurance. His spirit toppled. He had barely dipped his toe into adulthood and he already wished he could go back.

"All you have to do is go to the bank to apply for one. You ought to have one. They're great for emergencies."

Sam perked up. He could see the wisdom in that. Surely, his grandpa would too. Not that he would necessarily bring it up to Grandpa. No use stirring him up if he didn't have to. Besides, if he had to pay adult bills, he should be able to enjoy a bit of the freedom along with it.

They stepped into another store with a cosmetic counter at the front.

"Would you like to try our new men's fragrance?" The woman who stood before them had a flawless complexion, thick dark curls that coiled around her shoulders, and brown almond-shaped eyes.

How could they refuse? Sam and Jake stepped over to the counter and allowed her to spray a light burst of the scent on their wrists.

"This is nice," Jake said with a smile at the woman who smiled back. He turned to Sam. "Don't you think so?"

"Yeah, real nice." Sam did like the scent. It made him think of camp and hiking in the woods.

"We'll take two," Jake announced with a wide grin, handing the woman his credit card.

The clerk was obviously pleased with making a quick sale. She told them she'd be back in a moment.

"What are you doing? I don't have enough money for that," Sam protested.

"I'm buying. You can buy me something once you get your credit card. With the credit card paying your bills, it leaves you a little cash in your pocket." He winked.

When the woman came back with their purchases, she was still smiling. So was Jake. They thanked her and walked deeper into the store. The more Sam thought about it, the more he liked the idea of getting a credit card.

Yes, first chance he had, he planned to get one.

"WE DECIDED TO COME back home and hang out," Emily said when she stepped into the family room, Troy right behind her.

"Everything okay?" Bob asked, followed by a yawn. Charlotte was flooded with relief at seeing the kids at the front door.

"Everything is fine, Grandpa," Emily said.

Charlotte was dying to ask for details but decided to let Emily fill her in at her own pace. "How about some popcorn?"

"Sounds great." Emily turned to Troy. "Why don't you sit in here with Grandpa while Grandma and I get the popcorn."

Charlotte was almost certain she saw fear leap to Troy's eyes. "You'll be fine," she said with a smile.

In the kitchen, Charlotte and Emily set to work getting out bowls for the popcorn and glasses for drinks. Charlotte shoved the popcorn in the microwave and set the timer.

Her heart felt lighter just knowing Emily was home and everything was okay.

"So what made you decide against the movie?" Charlotte asked.

"It was rated R. Troy didn't know that. I told him I didn't want to see it."

Charlotte felt proud that Emily had opted not to see the movie. Many kids would have gone to it anyway. Charlotte smiled at her. "I'm proud of you."

"Thanks." Emily filled all the glasses with ice cubes and then poured tea.

"You know, Allison Cunningham said she saw you pulled over on the side of the road," Charlotte said, leaning against the sink counter while keeping an eye on the microwave popcorn. "Is there anything else I should know?"

"No, Grandma," Emily answered. "Troy thought he ran over a dead animal so we got out to make sure the tires were okay. Maybe that's when Mrs. Cunningham drove by."

"Well, I figured she was just trying to find trouble," Charlotte replied. "I'm glad it was nothing to worry about."

"Me too."

The popcorn finished popping and Charlotte emptied the bag into a large bowl. With a smile, she turned to Emily. "Now, let's go rescue your boyfriend from Grandpa."

Chapter Eight

Christopher and Dylan were up with the chickens at the crack of dawn on Saturday. They shoved through the back door, lured by the smell of hot biscuits fresh out of the oven, sausage and gravy bubbling in a large skillet on the stove, and fried eggs sizzling on Grandma's griddle.

"Smells so good, Grandma."

She turned to them with a smile, wearing her white and blue checkered apron, the very garment Christopher most liked to see on his grandma.

"You boys go get washed up for breakfast, and I'll get it on the table while you're getting ready."

They scrambled to get to the bathroom.

"I'm starving," Dylan said, plunging his soapy hands beneath the faucet.

"Me too."

"Your grandma is a good cook."

"She's the best." Christopher dried his dripping hands on the hanging towel.

"Hey, you don't think we have to worry about that initiation thing today, do you?" Dylan asked, right eye twitching.

Christopher hardly noticed his friend's tics now. Tourette's syndrome was a part of Dylan's life and Christopher had grown used to it. He did notice, however, that stress made it worse.

"Nah. I think Uncle Pete was just trying to worry us. He's like that. My sister says they don't do initiations into youth groups." Christopher prayed she was right—only his prayer was much shorter than Grandpa's.

Christopher's response seemed to put Dylan at ease. He didn't say any more about it as they made their way to the kitchen for breakfast.

"I figured you boys had better have a hearty breakfast since you'll be working hard today," Grandma said, sliding two fried eggs onto each of their plates while the boys brought the bowls of sausage gravy and biscuits to the table.

"Sure smells good in here," Grandpa said, joining them at the table. "Where are the other two kids?"

"Emily had a headache this morning, so I let her sleep in since she's working at Bill's house later today. And Sam got a late start. He's outside milking Trudy. We'll have to start without him."

Grandpa nodded and said grace. Christopher tried to concentrate, but sometimes his grandpa's prayer seemed to travel the globe before it landed back at their breakfast table. He breathed in the breakfast smells, wanting desperately to dig in, and praying a prayer of his own that Grandpa would stop praying. He knew it was a selfish prayer and most likely wouldn't get answered, but Pastor said the Bible says, "Ye have not because ye ask not," or something like that. Anyway, he figured it didn't hurt to ask.

"Amen," Grandpa said.

To which Dylan and Christopher both responded with a hearty "amen." Next, the boys dug their forks into their plates with gusto.

"I suppose you boys are looking forward to the youth event today?" Grandpa said.

"We sure are," Christopher said.

Dylan nodded while chomping on a biscuit.

"What time are you supposed to meet at the church again?" Grandma said.

"We're supposed to be there in forty-five minutes," Christopher said, before taking a bite of sausage gravy.

"We have time then," she said.

"I reckon Grandma and I will have to read devotions on our own this morning. You two will, no doubt, hear some Scriptures once Pastor Vink gets ahold of you."

Christopher smiled, feeling great relief. Prayer was one thing, but Christopher could grow whiskers by the time Grandpa got through devotions.

Once breakfast was over, Grandma drove them to the church. When they arrived, most of the teens were already there. Christopher could feel his face flush. Nothing like everyone looking at them as they climbed out of the car.

He wished Emily had come. At least she could have paved the way for them. With her helping Uncle Bill today, Christopher and Dylan had to go it alone. At least they had each other to hang out with in case everyone treated them like losers.

Pastor Vink welcomed the new kids into the group and explained where they were going and what they would be doing for the day. After prayer, everyone was to load onto the church vans.

While making their way to the vans, Christopher was surprised how many kids said "hello" and welcomed them into the group.

He decided this was going to be a good day. Why he ever let Uncle Pete get to him with that initiation business, he'd never know.

"ARE YOU SURE you don't mind driving me to Aunt Anna's house, Grandma?"

"I'm sure. I'd like to do some window shopping in River Bend, so this gives me a good excuse. I thought you weren't supposed to help again until next week, though."

"That was the original plan. But Aunt Anna mentioned some things she wants done before then, so I offered to come over today. I'm glad she's letting me. I can use the money."

By the time Emily and her grandma arrived at Uncle Bill and Aunt Anna's house the sun had burned off the morning dew and settled high in the sky. The blistering heat had set in, promising another hot August day.

Grandma visited for a few minutes with Uncle Bill and Aunt Anna. Then she said goodbye, and Aunt Anna and Emily set to work.

Aunt Anna surveyed the kids' playroom. "Okay, we have children coming for a visit this week, so my thought was to have you clean the play area. Basically, I want you to drag the plastic, washable toys into the bathroom, and wash them in the bathtub. Just a little light work today."

If she thought this was light work, Emily didn't even want to think about what heavy-duty work was to her.

"Then once the toys are cleaned, I'd like you to organize them. The girls can show you which toys go in the toy chest, which ones belong on the shelves, that sort of thing. Sound good?" She flashed a smile.

"Yeah," Emily said, lifting a forced smile in return. In truth, she had just told a fib. It didn't sound good to her at all. She wasn't allergic to work, but Aunt Anna drove her crazy with her precise ways. No doubt Emily would wash the toys and they wouldn't be clean enough or disinfected enough to her satisfaction, but whatever. She needed the money and that was that.

SAM DROVE HIS CAR into the grocery parking lot and cut the engine. He didn't mind picking up a few things for his grandma. He'd had his fun last night, so that helped. Otherwise, he'd be moping around all day because he was spending a fine Saturday doing errands.

A girl passed him in the grocery and smiled. He wondered if it was that new cologne. He took a whiff of his arm. It still smelled pretty good. He glanced again at the girl, who glanced back at him with another smile. He wasn't one to wear cologne, but maybe he should rethink that.

"Hey, Sam, how's it going?"

Sam turned around to see a couple of guys from high school.

"Hey, guys. What's up?"

"We're getting some grub to take to Aaron Green's house for a barbecue tonight. Want to come?" Wilson Smith rubbed his jaw, grinned, and gave a wink. "Aaron's folks will be gone, so we'll have the place all to ourselves."

All Sam could think about was the trouble he'd gotten into the last time he'd gone to a party where there were no parents. He merely smiled. "Sounds tempting, but I've got to get things ready for school. Where you guys going this year?"

Bobby South spoke up. "Oh man, no way I'm going back to school. Why wait four years? I'm making good money right now."

"What kind of work are you doing?"

"Construction. That's where the big money is," Bobby said. "We each got ourselves an apartment, car, money to spare." He nodded his head with confidence.

"That's great."

"So you're headed back to school?" Bobby asked, and before Sam could respond, he said, "Bummer. I'd rather get on with my life than waste four years in school, listening to some boring teacher drone on about something I don't want to hear about."

"Yeah, I know," Sam said, feeling gloomier by the minute.

"Dude, we feel for ya," Wilson said with a pat on the arm. "If you want to come to the party, it starts at six-thirty. You know where Aaron lives, right?"

"Yeah. Thanks."

"Hope you can make it."

The two moved on, leaving Sam to watch after them. No school. The very thought of it energized him. To be free to do what he wanted, make money, not have homework. He could only imagine.

Did those guys have any idea how lucky they were? The bigger question was, could he be that lucky?

CHRISTOPHER PLOPPED DOWN on his beach towel on the banks of Heather Creek. The breeze did little to ease the heat. He could hardly wait to plunge into the cool water.

Everyone gathered on the bank, eagerly awaiting Pastor Vink's signal to jump in, but instead he walked in front of them with the prettiest girl Christopher had ever seen in his life.

"Hey, gang, I'd like to introduce you to Bailey Winters. She comes to us from Indiana. Her family just moved to Bedford last week, and I've invited her for the swimming part of our activity today since she's spent all week helping her family move into their new home. I hope you'll make her feel welcome."

Bailey had a smile that made him think of the moon on a starry night. Not only that but when she smiled, it caused crickets to jump around in Christopher's stomach. Maybe he was getting sick or something. Her long brown hair lifted gently in the breeze and settled around her arms like his sister's silky scarf. Christopher caught himself gaping and quickly closed his choppers. He turned to Dylan and caught his friend staring at him with a stupid grin.

"What?" Christopher asked.

Dylan covered his mouth to keep from laughing out loud.

"Did you have something to say, Dylan?" Pastor Vink asked, causing Christopher's breath to come to a complete standstill and hover just around his chest.

Dylan blinked. "Um, no."

"Oh, I thought you said something." Pastor turned to the group. "Well, okay, then. What are you waiting for? Let's get cooled off!"

The older kids yelled and scrambled to get to the water, splashing and thrashing about. Christopher sat perfectly still, trying to get his heart back into normal rhythm. A couple of girls went over to Bailey and talked to her, and then they went in the water. He wanted to welcome her to the group. That would be the Christian thing to do, after all.

Christopher took a deep breath and walked toward her. His heart pounded so hard, he was afraid someone would hear it. Once he reached her, the worst thing happened. His tongue stuck to the roof of his mouth. All moisture gone.

"Hi," she said with a killer smile.

Christopher swallowed hard. Then he swallowed hard again.

"Hi. I'm Christopher," he finally managed.

"Bailey."

"Um, welcome to the group."

"Thanks." Her eyes were shiny like her hair. He wondered how she did that.

"What grade are you in?" he asked.

"Seventh."

"Me too. Maybe we'll have some classes together."

"Maybe."

Just then some of the girls came up to her again and Christopher said goodbye, but not before tripping over a hunk of weeds in his path. At least he didn't fall, and he didn't look back to see if she had noticed. He heard some giggles, though, which only added to his misery.

He brushed it off. Enough of this girl stuff. He ran to the water and joined Dylan.

But once he hit the water, he decided nothing was more refreshing than Bailey's smile.

"OKAY, THE PLAYROOM looks pretty good. I'd like you to go over that toy trunk, though. I can still see smudges on the brass closure."

Emily took a deep breath and tried to hide her frustration.

"Another thing. Do you have plans for tonight?"

Emily was wishing with all her might that she had had plans, but unfortunately, she didn't. "No."

"Great. I got to thinking that since you're here it might be a good time to go clean out my cookbooks and cupboards in the kitchen. I've just got way too many dishes. We'll ask your grandma when she comes to get you if I can take you home later. You'll eat dinner with us, of course." She whipped around and left the room, leaving Emily bummed.

After Emily had finished with the trunk and was satisfied

that the room sparkled, she walked into the living room just as her aunt opened the door to Grandma. She heard them discussing Aunt Anna's latest venture.

Grandma glanced up and saw her. "There you are, Emily. Are you all right with staying and helping Anna tonight and her bringing you home later? I need to prepare dinner for the boys, and we have to pick up Christopher from the youth day."

"That's fine." What else could she say? It would be rude to say otherwise. She just had to deal with it. Still, that didn't mean she had to be happy about it.

"It's all settled then. We'll bring Emily home later." Aunt Anna spoke as though the matter was completely settled and it was time to move on.

"Well, okay, if you're sure," Grandma said, oblivious to the pain going through Emily. "See you later, dear," she said to Emily with a wave.

Emily waved and mustered a weak smile. She took a deep breath and tried to calm herself. Madison and Jennifer came into the room and distracted her with talk of a new book and Emily settled into the idea of sticking around for a few more hours. After all, it wasn't her cousins' fault that their mom was a neat freak.

Her aunt closed the door behind Grandma and turned to Emily. "Follow me to the kitchen and we can get started."

Emily could hardly wait.

In no time, dressed in a fancy apron, hair perfectly in place, Emily's aunt stood at the stove, stirring something in a skillet while doling out directions for sorting through myriad cookbooks.

"What are you fixing?" Emily asked, placing the books in different piles.

"Beef bourguignon." Aunt Anna, who was searing chunks of beef in hot oil, turned to her. "It's French cuisine."

Emily wondered if she would need to hold up her pinkie while she ate dinner tonight.

"I could actually use your help making it. Put those books aside and come over here."

Emily wondered how Uncle Bill could put up with her aunt's bossiness. Though she didn't like to touch meat, it appeared Emily didn't have any choice in the matter. She walked over to her aunt.

"Here. Cut up some carrots and onions. I'll need to put those in the oil and cook them." She handed Emily a knife that could most definitely sever a finger. She must have noticed Emily's wide eyes.

"Oh, you haven't used one of these before?"

Emily shook her head.

"It's quite simple, really." She demonstrated. "Just be careful and you'll be fine. It's when people don't pay attention that they get into trouble. You can't do two things at once when you're using these knives. Keep your mind on what you're doing."

Emily carefully and slowly cut up the carrots and onions, dabbing at her eyes with a tissue once she had finished.

"Those chunks are too big. I'd like you to slice them a little thinner," Aunt Anna said.

Emily reminded herself of the jeans. She needed jeans. She would get through this.

"I remember that you don't like meat, so I'll set aside a

bowl of stew for you without the meat. You'll be missing the best part, though," she said as though she didn't approve.

"Thanks," Emily said. *Jeans. New jeans.*

"That's better," Aunt Anna said when Emily showed her the new and improved cut vegetables. Aunt Anna threw them into the oil, and then added some other ingredients. Ultimately, it turned into a thick stew.

"I neglected to ask you how your babysitting class went."

Emily didn't want to talk about it. "It was fine. The teacher called and asked me to be her aide next week. I'm the oldest kid in the class." She tried not to sound bitter.

"Better to be older and know what you're doing."

Emily didn't say anything. It was just better that way. She turned her attention to rubbing bread with a cut clove of garlic and then toasting it in the oven.

While waiting for the bread to toast, Aunt Anna shared a couple of stories of her babysitting days. Sometimes Emily wondered if Aunt Anna ever messed up on anything.

"It's ready," Emily said, pulling the bread from the oven.

"Wonderful. We'll put the bread in here." Aunt Anna glanced at the bread. "It's a little dark, but it will have to do." She handed Emily a dish lined with a linen cloth. "Just fold that over the bread once you put it in there."

She called her family to dinner, lit the candles in the center, and filled all the glasses with iced tea, and then Emily surveyed the table. In that moment, she realized that while perfectionism was high on her aunt's list, she expected the same perfection from herself as she did from others.

Uncle Bill said the prayer and dishes were passed.

"When you have time, I'll teach you a few things about gourmet cooking."

Emily wasn't sure how she felt about being stuck in a kitchen with Aunt Anna. "Um, sure."

"Uh-oh," Uncle Bill said. "Beware, Emily. She'll never let you out of the kitchen." He chuckled, reaching for a piece of bread.

Shivers ran up Emily's spine.

"By the way, did you get that trunk polished?"

"Yes."

"Good. I'll look around and see what your next project will be."

Aunt Anna was getting on her nerves. The jeans were quickly losing their appeal.

Chapter Nine

"Everything checks out all right, Charlotte." A shiny silver and black stethoscope dangled around Dr. Carr's neck, as he stood before her in his white coat.

Seemed to Charlotte that the weekend had passed in a blur, so it relieved her greatly to hear Dr. Carr's words. Charlotte shrugged. "Wish I knew why I was so tired all the time."

Dr. Carr looked her squarely in the eyes. "You're not thirty anymore, Charlotte. You still try to do the work of a thirty-year-old."

She grinned. "I suppose so."

"You need some time for you." He reached for his pad. "So I'm writing you a prescription for rest and I'm giving you the name of a new multivitamin I'd like you to try. I think you'll see a bit of improvement once you start taking this supplement."

He ripped a page off the pad and handed it to her with a smile that quickly turned to a look of concern. "I want you to get some rest. If you don't take care of yourself, no one will. You can't help the family if you're sick."

She nodded, trying not to cry. Her emotions seemed at the surface these days too.

Dr. Carr patted her shoulder. "Go on that trip with Hannah."

She looked up in surprise. "How did you . . ."

"We live in a small town, remember? When one of our own wins something, we hear about it." He grinned.

"Got to love small town living."

"Well, you go on that trip and enjoy yourself. You've earned it. Then come back refreshed and ready to work again. You know what Pastor says: 'Even Jesus had to get away now and then.'"

Charlotte bid Dr. Carr goodbye, received her paperwork, and headed out the door.

Somehow the sunshine seemed a little brighter, the air a little cooler, the birdsong a little more lively when she pushed through the doors of the clinic and walked to her car. Tears misted her eyes. Charlotte knew deep in her heart that she had been a little worried about what the doctor would say. She wasn't used to feeling so tired. She hoped the vitamins would help.

Once Charlotte got home, she invited Hannah over for tea and told her what the doctor had said.

"I'm glad you went to see the doctor. Now maybe you'll stop worrying," Hannah said.

The way Hannah was speaking made Charlotte feel she'd been reprimanded. "I'm not worried, Hannah, I'm just tired."

"Well, whatever it is, maybe you'll stop complaining and enjoy the gift of going with me."

Charlotte opened her mouth to respond but the words

stuck in her throat. She hadn't been complaining, had she? Hannah's tone was a bit confrontational, and Charlotte didn't appreciate it at the moment.

They finished their coffee and tea in silence.

BOB WALKED THROUGH the back door and kicked off his boots as Charlotte put the finishing touches on dinner.

"Just in time," she said, placing the stoneware plates on place mats around the table. "The kids talked me into tacos tonight, I hope you don't mind." The thump of plates on place mats filled the moment between them. "I went to the doctor today, and you were right—everything is fine. Turns out I just need some rest and a multivitamin." With one look at his tired face, she didn't bother to mention her little tiff with Hannah. Besides, it would blow over soon enough. Hannah had probably had a bad day and was a tad touchy. Charlotte walked over to Bob and looked up at him. "You okay?"

"I'm fine," he said in a tone that indicated he wasn't fine at all. He kissed the top of her head. "I'll get washed up for dinner." His heavy footsteps told her they'd all better tread lightly during dinner. Bob needed a little extra grace and compassion tonight. At least she'd baked another apple pie.

"This grub is awesome, Grandma," Sam said, once they started eating.

She looked at him and chuckled. "Thank you." She was glad to see at least someone was in a good mood at the table tonight. With all these mood swings, she wondered if there was a full moon.

"Sorry I'm late," Emily said, dashing in through the back door. "Ashley and I lost track of time. I'll get washed up." She ran through the kitchen before anyone could comment. Given Bob's current humor, it was probably a good thing.

If there was one thing Bob didn't tolerate well it was children being late for dinner. He shared Charlotte's view that the family should sit down to dinner together whenever possible. Amazingly enough, he didn't comment when Emily came through the door. In fact, he looked preoccupied.

Charlotte glanced at Christopher and watched as he pushed the taco meat around on his plate with the fork. He'd taken only one bite.

"Christopher, don't you feel well?"

He shrugged. "I'm okay. Just not real hungry."

Alarm shot through Charlotte. She had never once seen him turn down tacos. Something was seriously wrong with him. Emotional or physical, she couldn't tell . . . yet.

The way Bob bit into his taco said he had an ax to grind. Something must have happened at work. Maybe he'd had a run-in with a customer or maybe even with Andy Weber. After overhearing Andy bark out orders the other day, she wondered how things were going. Both men were strong willed and both were used to being in charge. Could this be the problem? On the other hand, Bob had a heart of gold when it came to helping others out, so she couldn't imagine him letting Andy's ways get to him. After all, the man was old and dealing with Parkinson's. That was enough to make anyone snappy. Surely, Bob would understand that.

"How's it going at the store, Grandpa?" Sam asked, reaching for another taco shell and piling it high with fixings.

"All right." Bob's curt words prompted no further discussion about it.

Emily slid into her chair and grabbed a taco. Just as she started to eat, Bob looked at her.

"You weren't here for grace. You'd best be sure to thank the Lord for your food. Plenty of people don't have such a luxury. Don't take it for granted."

"Yes, Grandpa." Emily bowed her head and closed her eyes a moment or two before eating.

Charlotte wanted to keep the conversation at dinner light and happy, but the air was tense. Everyone seemed to notice but Sam. She couldn't figure out what his happy mood was about, but she was thankful. Lately, all he thought about was school and how much he didn't want to go. Maybe he'd finally come to terms with it.

"So do you have all your books for school now, Sam?" Charlotte asked.

"All but two. I was trying to buy them online at a discount, but I don't think it's gonna happen. I've contacted two other students who posted books on a bulletin board at school. They're trying to sell them since they don't need them anymore, and I hope to get them from them rather than the bookstore."

"I see," Charlotte said.

"It's ridiculous what they charge kids for books that they'll use for one class," Bob said. He shoved a spoonful of ground meat into his taco.

"Yes, it's too bad it has to cost so much. I suppose everything's gone up these days," Charlotte said.

"That's no excuse," Bob said.

Emily ate her taco in silence.

Christopher had managed another bite, with no more interest in his food than if he'd just been told he had to take a bath.

"So how do you like being in the teen group, bro?" Sam asked.

Christopher said nothing, just kept his fork moving on his plate.

Everyone looked at him.

Sam nudged him. "Hey, nerd."

Christopher looked up. "What?"

Sam looked surprised. "Didn't you hear me?"

"What?" Christopher blinked.

"I asked how you liked the teen group?"

"Good. It's good. I really like it."

Sam studied him. "You all right?"

"Hm? Yeah, I'm fine. Fine."

Emily watched him too, but kept silent.

Whatever was going on with Christopher, everyone seemed at a loss. Maybe he would make them privy to it soon. But for now, his actions remained a mystery.

Anytime her grandson had a loss of appetite—which didn't happen often—it caused Charlotte grave concern.

CHRISTOPHER YANKED on his pajamas and crawled into bed. Tucking his hands behind his head, he stared upward to where Bailey Winters's face flashed across the ceiling. She was smiling again, causing another stir in the pit of his stomach. She wouldn't have the least bit of interest in him, he was sure, but he couldn't stop thinking about her.

He'd never been interested in girls before, so he wasn't sure about it all. He wanted to talk to Sam, but he was afraid Sam would make fun of him. But who else could he talk to? Dylan knew he thought Bailey was pretty, but he didn't really want to talk to Dylan about it either. He wasn't exactly "in the know" when it came to girls.

Grandpa had been out of commission far too long where women were concerned, so he was out. Uncle Pete had just gotten married, so women and dating might still be fresh on his mind. Maybe he'd be a good one to go to for some insight. He'd never really considered Uncle Pete an expert on girls and dating, but then his choices were limited. He'd have to take what he could get.

His eyelids grew heavy and he slowly surrendered to sleep, Bailey Winters's image following him into a magical world where dreams come true.

⌣ Chapter Ten

There was a spring in Sam's step as he made his way to the bank. He felt like an adult. What was he thinking? He *was* an adult, and it was time he started reaping the benefits of being one. If he was old enough for the military, he was old enough to get his own credit card—whether Grandpa agreed or not.

The bank personnel quickly met with him, had him fill out some paperwork, and gave him a temporary card to use till the permanent one came in the mail. He hoped his grandparents wouldn't get to the mail before he did and suspect anything. After all, he was of age, and it was his business, pure and simple.

Armed with a temporary card, Sam drove over to Harding to browse the stores. Not that he was in need of anything in particular, but it didn't hurt to look and see if something popped up that he might need and just hadn't thought about up to now.

His grandparents didn't question his every move these days, which helped a little. Finally, they were granting him some breathing room. Grandma knew he was preparing for school that was scheduled to start in less than a week, so she assumed he was shopping for the last two books he needed for classes.

Thinking about those last two books made him remember that he wasn't at all happy that he had to take a music appreciation class. Was he interested in eighteenth-century monks singing their chants? No. But there he was, doomed to a full semester of arias and chants and who knew what else. His friends would be listening to their usual music and there he would be stuck in a class like that. It was so unfair. He didn't see how that would help him in his future life at all. But obviously, he had no choice in the matter. That's why he had decided to take it and get it out of the way. "No use putting off the inevitable," his mother used to say. Now he was finally old enough to understand what that meant.

Pushing through the doors of the mall, Sam sauntered from store to store, enjoying his newfound freedom. Though money didn't jangle in his pocket, his temporary credit card was burning a hole and he felt he had the world at his fingertips.

"I BROUGHT SOME BROCHURES of the Appleton Bed-and-Breakfast to look at while we take our break this morning," Hannah said, sliding into her chair.

"Oh, great." Charlotte poured herself a cup of coffee and Hannah a cup of tea, then set the saucers and cups in their places. Obviously, Hannah was feeling better than the last time they had talked.

"Just look at these rooms, Charlotte, aren't they lovely?"

Charlotte looked at the page showing rooms decorated with quilts, lanterns, cozy wallpaper and plump, overstuffed pillows. It all beckoned to her to relax and rest. She sighed and sipped slowly from her cup.

"It looks so inviting," Charlotte said.

"Doesn't it, though." Hannah looked at the brochure with a wistful gaze. "I can hardly wait to go there." She looked up at Charlotte. "I'm so glad you're going with me. We'll have a wonderful time, Charlotte. I just know we will."

"Yes, I believe we will," she agreed. "I'm truly looking forward to it."

"You are? It's about time. I was afraid I would have to take someone else."

That comment caused a ping to Charlotte's chest. Why would Hannah say such a thing?

"Well, you could always do that, if you'd prefer, Hannah," Charlotte said, feeling a tad put out.

"No. I asked you, and if you're willing to go, then I'm happy. I just don't want to drag you against your will." Hannah stirred some sugar into her cup.

Hannah was making her mad, pure and simple. Charlotte forced her mouth to her coffee cup lest she say something she shouldn't.

"I'm not trying to be harsh, Charlotte. It's just that this is a very special weekend, and I want to be with someone who will enjoy it with me. I had hoped that would be you."

"I said I want to go, Hannah." Charlotte could hear the edge in her voice, but she was only human, after all.

"Good. If you change your mind, though, just let me know."

Was that a threat that she could be uninvited?

Just then the air-conditioning kicked in, which was a

good thing. Charlotte could feel her inner temperature rising by the seconds.

"Oh, I almost forgot to tell you," Hannah said. "I was at the supply store this morning and Bob looked a little out of sorts. Is everything okay with him?"

Charlotte was glad Hannah had changed the subject, but wasn't at all sure this was the direction in which she wanted to go. "How so?" she asked.

Hannah shrugged. "Just the look on his face said he didn't want to be there."

"Well, you know, once you get into retirement, it's hard to go back into the workforce." Charlotte forced a chuckle, her fingers tracing the rim of her coffee cup.

"I'm sure that's right. Poor guy. Well, the good news is he doesn't have to do it for long, right?"

"Right. Brad will be home soon." Charlotte drained her cup. "I hope his family is enjoying their vacation. Montana is such beautiful country."

"So I hear. But I wouldn't trade Bedford for any place," Hannah said.

"Me, neither."

Charlotte glanced at Hannah and prayed nothing would ever change between them. She was the one true friend that Charlotte felt sure she could always count on.

SAM COULDN'T BELIEVE his good luck. To find all those clothes on sale was just too good to be true. Jeans, T-shirts, socks, a couple of pairs of shoes. He was all set for school now. He didn't have to feel like such a dweeb.

He carried his packages to the car and tried to figure

out a way to get them into the house without a lecture from his grandparents. Stuffing the bags in the trunk, he kept one bag holding two pairs of jeans on the front seat. He'd just take things in one at a time over a period of a few days—or he'd wait until his grandparents went somewhere and then he'd take the stuff up to his room.

He bet other kids didn't have to worry about such things. Sometimes his grandparents were so old-fashioned.

When he drove his car into the driveway, he noticed his grandpa's truck was gone. That made him feel better. Most likely, Grandpa was working at the supply store, which suited Sam just fine. Turning off the engine, he grabbed his package and headed inside.

Once he stepped through the back door, he saw Grandma in the kitchen, standing over the stove as usual. She turned to him while stirring something in a pot.

"Well, looks like somebody has had a good day."

Sam shrugged. "Just some jeans for school."

"Great," she said. "That money from your uncle comes in handy once in a while, doesn't it?" She stirred whatever was on the stove.

"Um, yeah." He tried to get past her, but she was in a chatty mood.

"I know you don't always enjoy working there, but when it helps with the books and clothes, it makes it all worthwhile."

"Yeah." He turned to go.

"Well, aren't you going to show me your jeans?"

Was she kidding? Why did he have to do that? It was such a girl thing to do.

"They're just jeans, Grandma."

She looked surprised and he felt a twinge of guilt. "All right, I'll show you," he said, pulling a pair of jeans from the crisp package. He was careful to hide the price tag.

"Oh my, those are nice," she said, reaching for them.

He backed away.

"Is something wrong?"

"No, I just need to straighten my room before dinner." He winced inwardly. She wouldn't buy that one. She knew good and well he wouldn't rush off to clean his room. He heard her gasp and he whirled back around.

"What's wrong?"

"You didn't pay that much for those jeans, did you?" She held her hand to her chest as though she might fall over any moment.

Without thinking, he grabbed the price tag and tucked it back in the jeans. "Oh, they were having a big sale today." Which was true—they were.

"Oh, good," she said, no doubt allowing her breath to kick back into its usual rhythm. "For a minute there—well, I should have known better. You kids are doing such a great job with managing your money. I wish my kids had been so wise at your age."

"Was Mom good with money?" He wasn't sure why he asked that. He needed to get upstairs and get off the subject of these jeans, but curiosity got the better of him.

"Heavens no. She got a credit card when she was much too young, and had the financial stress to prove it. We didn't know until she was already in over her head." Charlotte let out a regretful sigh. "We tried to help her, but your grandpa didn't want to make it too easy on her. He

wanted to teach her the lesson of financial responsibility."
She washed a small spot tomato sauce off her arm, then
turned off the faucet. "He was right, of course. If left to me,
I would have taken care of everything and she never would
have learned."

"Did she?"

She looked up at him with a start.

"Learn, I mean? Did she learn how to handle her
finances?"

A shadow crossed his grandma's face. "I don't know."

He nodded and then left the kitchen. The wooden steps
creaked as he made his way up the stairs to his room.

AFTER DINNER the kids went to their rooms and Bob
settled into his chair and turned on the TV with very little
discussion. He obviously was not in the mood to talk.
Charlotte was in the mood for ice cream, but when she
checked the freezer, there was no sign of ice cream anywhere. She checked every crevice.

"I'm going to town to pick up some ice cream," she told
Bob. "Do you want anything?"

"Get some chocolate syrup while you're at it," he said.

"Okay. Be right back." She grabbed her purse and walked
to her car. She'd get him chocolate syrup, all right—
sugar-free chocolate syrup. She wasn't about to contribute
to his diabetes problem.

The evening air held a hint of damp. Charlotte looked
up and saw clouds forming. No doubt they'd be getting
rain showers tonight. The clouds were slowly gathering, so

hopefully she'd have time to get to the store and back before the downpour.

Once she walked into the store, she'd no sooner arrived at the frozen goods section when the sound of a squeaky cart approached and someone tapped her on the shoulder.

"Well, hello, Charlotte."

Charlotte turned to see Allison Cunningham standing behind her. Perfectly put together from her tailored navy suit down to her fashionable matching shoes, Allison stood with an eager smile that could only mean one thing. She was in the mood to talk.

Dressed in jeans and an everyday top, Charlotte would have preferred to turn around and walk away. "Hello, Allison."

"So we had a fine time at Hannah and Frank's the other night," Allison said, getting right down to business.

"That's good."

Allison picked up a package of frozen vegetables and pretended to study it. "Yes, she told me all about your girls' weekend getaway." Allison looked up and smiled. "She also said you were hesitant to go."

Charlotte didn't appreciate Allison's patronizing tone, nor did she appreciate that Hannah had shared that bit of information with Allison, of all people.

"Well, not dragging my feet exactly—"

Allison turned a vegetable package over in her hand and looked up again. "Not to worry, Charlotte. We're all starting to feel our age. I don't blame you at all. Those weekend getaways are for the young. She said if you changed your mind, she'd just ask someone else." Allison lifted a delicate

hand in the air and said, "No doubt someone younger."
Another chuckle.

Charlotte could feel the steam rising inside her and
prayed for strength not to blow right here and now.

"Well, you take care. So good to see you again." With a
dainty wave, she walked away.

Charlotte struggled with everything in her not to say
something unkind.

She fumed. How dare Hannah talk to this woman behind
Charlotte's back. She wasn't too old to go on a trip like this.
She just hadn't felt herself lately—was that so wrong? She
didn't think it was because of her age. Was it?

No matter. Hannah still shouldn't have been discussing
it with Allison. Now Charlotte wasn't at all sure she wanted
to go. Maybe she would back out and if Hannah wanted to
invite someone younger, so be it.

Chapter Eleven

Emily's jaw tensed when she walked into the bright, sterile room for the babysitting class and saw all the younger girls, their eyes revealing their insecurities. She so did not want to be there.

"Ah, good morning, Emily," Mrs. Hill said, kind smile in place. "I have some papers I'd like you to pass out for me." She padded over to Emily and handed her a small stack of papers.

While Emily passed out the papers, Mrs. Hill said, "Ladies, today we will learn how to perform the Heimlich maneuver and CPR. With little ones, you never know when they might put something down their throats that could get lodged there. It's our job to protect them from themselves. First, I will show you this DVD," she said, sliding the disk into the machine and turning it on, "then we'll discuss it afterward."

Mrs. Hill walked over to Emily and whispered, "Watch it closely. I'll want you to help me demonstrate once it's over."

Emily nodded. She wasn't intimidated by these girls at all, but she didn't know a lot about CPR or the Heimlich maneuver, so that made her nervous. She hoped she would be able to demonstrate it correctly.

Once the DVD had played through the demonstration, Mrs. Hill called Emily to the front and had her lie on a red mat on the floor. It was cool to the touch and Emily was glad because she was hot.

Mrs. Hill began, "Do not make a blind sweep of the child's mouth if she is choking. Make sure you can see what you're doing so you don't accidentally shove an object further down her windpipe. Many times the child can cough up the object on her own. However, if she can no longer speak, cough, or cry, you immediately set to work with the Heimlich maneuver to dislodge the foreign object."

Mrs. Hill demonstrated abdominal thrusts, talked of tilting the child's head to the side in case of vomiting, checking her mouth once more for the object, listening for breathing, and then, if necessary, following up with CPR.

The class listened intently and nodded.

She demonstrated once more. "Okay, so grab a doll over in that cabinet. Some are infants, some are older. We will talk about the differences in handling younger children versus older ones. I will walk around the room and when I get to you, I will want you to demonstrate for me how you would perform CPR on that child, if needed."

The girls excitedly ran over to the cabinet and began pulling out the dolls. Once each one had the doll of their choice, they settled onto mats on the floor to practice their procedures.

Mrs. Hill walked around the room. "You all are doing very well. I would feel confident leaving my child with you."

Emily thought her grandma should be there. She always worried that Will was choking on something or other. She loved her grandma but she fussed too much over the baby as far as Emily was concerned.

"Now, how to handle a child under the age of one." Mrs. Hill picked up an infant doll to demonstrate. She sat on a chair with the doll in her lap. "First, check to see if the child is breathing." She turned her ear toward the mouth of the doll. "If she is not breathing, gently turn her over, careful to support her neck and head, and give her up to five back slaps, not too hard, on her upper back with your hand. Turn her over and give her up to five chest thrusts. Repeat if necessary. If the baby is unresponsive, call 911 and then begin CPR."

All the while Mrs. Hill was demonstrating, Emily had cold chills. She couldn't imagine being in a situation like that. For sure she wouldn't have known what to do had she not taken this class. She vaguely remembered CPR from school, but it hadn't stuck with her.

The more she thought about it, the more she wondered if she really was ready to babysit—even at her age. Being a parent was a huge responsibility. She wasn't so sure she wanted to deal with that someday.

SAM PULLED HIS CAR up to the curb and let Christopher out. "I'll wait right here," he called out.

Christopher nodded and walked past the flowers bordering Bedford Community Church, then stepped inside the foyer. A copy machine whirred in the distance, which meant no doubt that Mrs. Ellis was working in the church office. He walked into the room.

Mrs. Ellis looked up. "Christopher," she said with a curt nod. His grandma had told him that Mrs. Ellis was a retired air-force lieutenant, and he believed her. With her cropped gray hair and sharp ways, Mrs. Ellis looked as though she were still in the military.

He wouldn't want to cross her.

She slipped the original paper from the copy machine and stacked the copies into a crisp tidy pile before placing them in a file on her desk.

"Hi, Mrs. Ellis. Is Pastor Vink in?"

"No. He'll be gone the rest of the afternoon," she said as she marched back to her desk.

Christopher scuffed the floor with his shoe. Sam was right—he should have come sooner. Now, it was likely too late to sign up for the team.

"Is there something I can help you with?"

"Nah. I wanted to sign up for the softball team before it was too late."

"That's no problem." She whipped out a clipboard with a sign-up sheet attached. "Just sign here."

He couldn't believe his good fortune. It wasn't too late to sign up for the softball team. Just wait till he told Sam. All this time his brother had probably been teasing him. When would Christopher learn not to listen to him? That's exactly why he couldn't talk to him about Bailey. Hard telling what Sam might put Christopher up to.

Christopher scrawled his name on the page, and then handed the pen back to Mrs. Ellis. "Thanks."

"You're welcome," she said. "Don't slouch your shoulders."

He immediately straightened and itched to follow up with a salute, though he restrained himself. When he turned around, there stood Bailey Winters in all her glory.

"Hi, Christopher," she said when she walked toward him.

The little men inside his head brought out the hammers. He tried to act nonchalant. He plunged a hand into his pocket to look cool and when he did, it threw him off balance. He tried to steady himself, but his hand got caught in a hole in his pocket, the hole he'd been meaning to tell Grandma about. Bailey looked at him and seemed to be holding back a laugh.

"Are you all right?"

The band of crickets and hammers thumped a steady staccato in his head, trumpets blared, and little bumps marched up his arms at the very sight of her.

Everything in him screamed to get out of there as fast as his legs could carry him.

He did.

HANNAH PULLED THE WEEDS and Charlotte lifted the ripe green beans from the vines in her vegetable garden. With irritation, Charlotte watched her. No doubt Hannah thought Charlotte too old to be out working in her garden. She wanted to bring the matter of Allison up to Hannah, but thought better of it. She would just sound like a jealous schoolgirl.

"So, you haven't changed your mind yet, have you— about the weekend getaway, I mean?" Hannah yanked on a stubborn weed, pulling it by the roots.

The more she had thought of it lately, the more Charlotte was committed to going. She wouldn't give Allison or anyone else the satisfaction of backing out so they could talk about how "old" she was.

"No. I told you I would go, and I will. I stand by my word." Charlotte dropped a handful of green beans into her basket.

Hannah shrugged. "Just wanted to give you the chance to back out if you wanted to."

"Well, I don't want to," Charlotte said, scooting along the ground, getting more irritated by the moment.

"You don't have to get mad about it. I just asked. I didn't want you to feel as though I was forcing you to go. This is a trip that's meant to be savored, not endured."

"I know. You've told me that a time or two."

"Well, it is."

Charlotte dusted off her hands. "Why do you act as though I don't appreciate your inviting me along?"

Hannah shrugged. "Well, you're the one who hemmed and hawed over the idea of going."

"You know I had my reasons, Hannah."

"Getting the kids ready for school? I mean, really, Charlotte, what kind of excuse is that?"

She locked her response behind clenched teeth.

Just then Sam's car drove into the driveway. Charlotte pushed herself up from the ground with a grunt, refusing to continue this pointless conversation with Hannah.

"I'd better make sure Sam got Christopher to church in time to sign up for the softball team."

"It's time for me to go home anyway. I'll talk to you later." Hannah stood up, brushed herself off, and then walked away.

"Thanks for your help," Charlotte called out.

Hannah merely waved, without looking back.

Obviously, Hannah was as miffed as Charlotte felt. She began to wonder just what kind of weekend getaway they were going to have.

Suddenly, Christopher bolted for the door. Charlotte looked at Sam as he sauntered over to her.

"What was that all about? Didn't he get signed up? Is he sick?" Charlotte asked, feeling the worry lines form on her forehead.

Sam's mouth split into a wide grin. "If you ask me, I think he's lovesick."

The words startled her. "Lovesick?"

Sam shrugged. "Just saying." He turned to walk off.

"Sam Slater, you turn back here this instant."

He turned around, smile still in place. "Yeah?"

"Who's he lovesick over? What makes you think it's that?"

"Think about it. He's been acting funny ever since he joined the teen group, right?"

"Right," Charlotte said, her mind spinning with the possibilities.

"Lost his appetite?"

"Yes." Sure, she'd noticed that too. But it was nervous butterflies over joining the youth group, wasn't it?

"Well, when he was at the church, this new girl walked in. I saw her. She's nice looking for a kid."

Charlotte might have thought Sam's older and wiser demeanor humorous were she not so concerned about Christopher.

"Go on."

"So she walks in and pretty soon, Christopher comes running out of the building, face white as a ghost, holding his stomach. He jumps in the car and says, 'Let's go.' I try to get him to talk about it, but no way. He's as close-mouthed as I've ever seen him. He's lovesick, all right."

"Well, who is this girl?" Charlotte wanted to know.

"I don't know. She's a new kid, as far as I can tell."

"How do you even know she had anything to do with Christopher? Maybe it was coincidental that she walked in there and he came out like that. Maybe something happened at the office."

"Trust me on this, Grandma. Christopher is experiencing his first crush."

With that, Sam walked away with a swagger if she'd ever seen one. Mr. Confidence himself most likely headed upstairs to give Little Brother some advice.

Charlotte was so not ready for this. Maybe she'd call Karen Ellis to see if she could shed some light on the matter.

Some days it just didn't pay to get out of bed.

Chapter
Twelve

Bob finished stocking the fuel pumps and straightened the shelves. He took a deep breath, turned around, and came face-to-face with Andy Weber.

"You need to remove a few of those so they don't take up too much shelf space," Andy said.

Bob clenched his teeth and lifted a few of the boxes from the shelves.

"Now that you've got that done, we just received a shipment of spark plugs in the back. The shelves are low, so you need to get 'em stocked," Andy said.

Bob had told himself over and over that Andy Weber had Parkinson's and Bob needed to have patience with the man. But Bob was nearing the end of his rope. Did the man have to bark out orders all day long?

Bob merely nodded.

"Go in the back room and get the boxes. They're clearly marked. I'll watch the register."

No one was in the store so they hardly needed anyone to man the register. Another deep breath and Bob stomped to the back room. All this physical activity was probably what kept him from giving Andy Weber a piece of his mind. But if things didn't ease up pretty soon, Bob was sure to blow.

"I'VE TRIED. I've really tried." Bob swung around to his wife. "You know I'm a patient man, Charlotte. But that Andy Weber is working me something powerful."

Charlotte watched her husband stomp across the kitchen floor, nostrils flared, arms swinging. She couldn't remember when she'd seen him so riled—except when he talked politics with Pete.

"What's wrong, Bob?"

He swung around to face her. "Andy Weber—that's what's wrong. I'm there to help him as a friend and he's bossing me around like I'm some oily-faced teenager." He paced some more. "I know how to work. I've run a farm for all these years. I don't need him telling me how to do things."

She wanted to point out that the store might be a little different than a farm but decided this might not be the right time. So she merely nodded.

More pacing. "I can handle customer orders and write up the forms. I'm familiar with the store and can help customers find things. Brad showed me how to run the register. No big deal." With every rant, his boots thumped against the floor and Charlotte could see where she'd have to mop up the scuff marks.

"Have you tried to talk to him?" she asked, gently.

He stopped in front of her again. "There is no talking to that man." He turned and stomped some more. "Now, I'm sorry he has Parkinson's, I really am, but I don't believe that's a good excuse for being rude to a friend."

"You're absolutely right, dear," Charlotte said.

He turned to her. "Don't patronize me, Charlotte. I'm upset."

"I can see that."

"Well, Brad had better hurry home quick—that's all I've got to say. Our years of friendship may fall apart before he gets home." With that, he stormed back outside and disappeared into the barn. He would find solace there. He always did.

Charlotte couldn't help lingering on his comment about their years of friendship falling apart. She hadn't realized until recently just how fragile friendships could be.

SAM PAID FOR HIS last textbook and put it in his car. The last two he had bought used which cost much less. He was happy about that. With the money he saved on the textbooks, he figured he could afford to pick up a couple of new tunes for his phone. Plus, putting it on his credit card gave him a whole month to save up for it.

He settled into his car seat and checked his hair in the mirror. He didn't want to look like a geek after all.

The more he thought about it, the more he liked the world of credit. He didn't see why his grandpa was so against it. If he paid the bill off at the end of each month, he wouldn't fall into debt and he'd be able to enjoy the purchase for that much longer.

He had figured all this out before he even started college. Life was good.

Walking through the department store in Harding, Sam spotted the latest phones and accessories. He browsed through the cases and headphones. He had goose bumps just looking at it all. He picked up a leather cover, a stylus, and a charger for the car. He'd go home and download some songs from the Internet. Man, this was awesome.

On his way out of the store, he spotted some car fresheners. He knew his car could use some of those, just in case he had to take a girl home or something. He grabbed a few to hang from his mirror.

Another stop at the checkout area. Another swipe of his card.

Holding his purchases, he swung through the exit door and walked toward his car with his head held high and an extra bounce in his steps. He couldn't believe all he'd been missing out on. This was living. Who said you can't enjoy life? He didn't have to deny himself stuff anymore. He'd still be careful. He wasn't stupid. But gone were the days of only spending his money on car and school expenses. He was going to start living a little!

The more he thought about it, the more he didn't mind his job at the law office. After all, that job made these purchases possible.

He was feeling so much better about things. If he decided not to stay in school, it was his choice. Might even look up his dad again. He felt like he had the world at his fingertips.

Yes, life was good.

EMILY COULDN'T BELIEVE she had made it through her last babysitting class. She was so relieved. She had hated being the oldest, but by today's class, she had grown used to the idea and decided it hadn't been so bad. Still, she was glad it was over.

While driving to Uncle Bill and Aunt Anna's house, her

thoughts turned to Troy. She'd hardly talked to him since their last date. He had left on Monday for his trip and would be gone about a week, so she'd just have to wait to hear from him.

She pulled her grandma's car up to her uncle's house and Madison let her inside. The house smelled of spicy herbs and baked bread. Emily followed her nose to the kitchen and found Aunt Anna there.

"Hi."

Aunt Anna was dressed in a stylish pair of boot-cut jeans, a crisp white blouse with appropriate jewelry and a pair of low heels. A mint green apron covered the front of her wide black belt and an oven mitt covered her right hand as she pulled bread from the oven.

She reminded Emily of the old reruns that her grandpa watched. What was that lady's name? Oh, yes, June Cleaver. Though Emily didn't think June Cleaver ever wore jeans.

"Wow, you look nice."

Aunt Anna turned, a wide smile on her face. She placed the perfectly shaped loaf of bread on the counter and closed the oven door. "Thank you."

"What's the occasion?"

"Oh, just thought I'd take the girls out this afternoon to celebrate your graduation from the babysitting course."

Wait. She graduated the course and they got to celebrate?

"I trust you'll be just fine with Will." Aunt Anna smiled sweetly, as though she'd just offered Emily a full ride to Harvard. Of course, to be fair, Emily supposed Aunt Anna considered baby Will worth far more than that, and in fact, she did too.

"Now, since Charlotte told me you didn't have an aversion to dairy products, I've made potato soup with thick slices of wheat bread for your dinner."

Emily's heart warmed at her aunt's thoughtfulness. "Thank you."

"My pleasure. When you're hungry, just help yourself. Since it will be an easy afternoon with the girls gone and Will taking a nap for a while, I would appreciate it if you would clean up the dishes and sweep the kitchen before he wakes up. Also, I have a load of laundry in the dryer. If you would fold the clothes the way I showed you last week that would be great."

Aunt Anna didn't just fold clothes—she made the process an art form. In fact, when she was done folding, the laundry looked like a class in origami.

"Okay." Emily tried not to reveal the sinking in her stomach. This woman never rested. True, she paid Emily well, but couldn't she give her a break now and then? If her home were any cleaner, they'd post it in a magazine.

Her aunt got the girls ready and they turned to leave. "By the way," she said, "I have a cookbook on vegetarian gourmet cooking, if you'd like to browse through it."

"Yeah, I would," Emily said eagerly.

"It's in the cabinet, over there." Aunt Anna pointed. "See you later."

Emily had to admit the kitchen cleanup didn't take as long as she had feared. She grabbed the cookbook and took it into the living room to browse through before Will woke up. Settling onto the sofa she thumbed through the pages. A glass of iced tea would taste good, she decided, so she went into the kitchen to prepare it. Fortunately, there was tea in the refrigerator. She poured herself a glass. When she tasted it, she winced. Evidently, Aunt Anna didn't care for sugar.

Emily rummaged through the cupboards for some sugar, added it to her tea, and then finally settled in the living room with her cookbook again. The combination of refreshing tea, plump cushions beneath her, the quiet of the house—all made her realize this job wasn't so bad after all. In fact, she decided, it was an easy way to get her jeans, now that the babysitting class was over. Aunt Anna had her moments, for sure, but today she wasn't so bad.

A contented sigh escaped Emily—until a cry from the baby's room let her know naptime was over, all too soon.

UNCLE PETE AND AUNT DANA had joined the family for dinner on the farm. Christopher kept watching Uncle Pete while the grown-ups talked among themselves. He really wanted to get advice on girls but wondered if Uncle Pete would laugh at him.

His palms started to sweat and his heart hammered against his shirt. He wanted to get it over, but wasn't sure how to go about it.

"Got any cookies, Mom?" Uncle Pete asked.

"You know I have cookies. What kind of mother would I be if I didn't keep my cookie jar filled?" She laughed. "Go help yourself to the peanut butter cookies."

"Thanks. Want some?" he asked Aunt Dana.

But she shook her head no. Christopher could never

understand why anyone would turn down a perfectly good cookie. And his grandma's peanut butter cookies were one of his favorites!

Cookies sounded like a good idea to Christopher, so he seized the opportunity to follow Uncle Pete into the kitchen.

Uncle Pete pulled a plate from the cabinet and plunged his hand deep into the cookie jar. Pulling out four or five, he put them on the plate, grabbed a glass of cold milk and sat down at the table.

"Hey, you gonna join me, Christopher?"

"I think I will." Christopher gathered a handful of cookies and sat down.

"So what's on your mind?" Uncle Pete asked with a grin.

"Who said there was anything on my mind?" Christopher wondered if his uncle was psychic or something.

"It's been pretty obvious. You've watched my every move tonight as though you wanted to say something but weren't sure when to jump in. I didn't want to ask you in front of the others in case it was private." He dunked a cookie in his glass of milk. "So what is it?"

Christopher swallowed past the boulder in his throat and then he took a deep, deep breath. "Well, there's this, um, girl."

Uncle Pete's eyes grew as wide as his cookies. "Oh?"

Christopher almost wished he hadn't said anything, but they were having a manly moment and he figured he'd better not let it escape.

"There's this girl in the youth group, and she's really pretty."

"Uh-huh."

Christopher glanced up now and then to make sure Uncle Pete wasn't laughing at him. He wasn't.

"Well, I've never had a girlfriend before, and I don't know what to do."

"I see." Uncle Pete downed the last bite of his cookie and finished his milk while Christopher waited. Finally, he leaned back in his chair, causing the front legs to lift from the floor. "It's like this, Christopher. Girls like boys who are manly. The best way to get a girl to notice you is to show your best skills. Run faster, play ball harder, act like a man. She'll be so impressed, she'll want you to notice her."

"Is that what happened with you and Aunt Dana?"

Pete's chair dropped to the floor. "Well—" he stopped to cough, "—something like that. Didn't you just sign up for the softball team?"

Christopher nodded.

"There you go. Impress her with how you play. Next thing you know, she'll be cheering for you. Don't act like a geek. Be tough. Splash on a little cologne. They like older dudes. It's all in the manly thing. Got it?"

Christopher thought for a moment. That made sense to him. "Thanks, Uncle Pete."

Pete grinned and pushed away from the table. "Good luck, kid." He ruffled the top of Christopher's hair and walked away.

Christopher sure wished grown-ups would stop doing that.

He rinsed out their plates and glasses and put them in the dishwasher. Then he went upstairs to his bedroom.

Closing the door, Christopher locked it so no one could come in.

Standing in front of the mirror, he stared at his reflection. He curled his arms to form tight muscles. They were barely a blip on the screen to his way of thinking. He thought Sam had some small weights—maybe he'd let Christopher try them out. He leaned into the mirror and zeroed his focus on his upper lip. Smooth as a baby's bottom. He didn't really know about that, but he had heard Uncle Pete use that phrase more than once when talking about a bald man at church. No, Christopher would have to think of another way to look older.

He ventured over to Sam's room and knocked on the door.

"What's up?" Sam asked when he opened the door.

"I was wondering if I could borrow your weights sometime," Christopher said, spotting them in the corner of Sam's room.

Sam smiled, though Christopher wasn't sure why, and said, "Sure. I haven't used them in a while. Take them to your room."

"Really?"

"Really."

Christopher's heart nearly darted from his chest. He went over to the ten-pound weights and picked them up, letting out a groan. Okay, not that heavy, but well, they were heavy. He straightened his back and acted like it was no big deal while Sam watched him go to his room. He heard Sam's chuckle when he closed the door of his own room, barely making it to his bed before he dropped the weights.

Mature men had muscles. That would convince Bailey even if his softball skills didn't.

After getting ready for bed, Christopher said goodnight to everyone and climbed into bed. Uncle Pete's words played back in his head. He'd practice running and swinging the bat every single day so he could do a good job when Bailey watched from the bleachers. And if he developed real muscles, he'd whack that softball out of the county. The very idea made him smile as he snuggled into his covers.

Chapter
Thirteen

It was a good thing Christopher wasn't superstitious or he wouldn't want to play ball in front of Bailey on Friday the thirteenth. Fortunately, it was only practice.

He looked around the stands at the softball field. Some kids walked onto the field. Girls climbed onto the bleachers. He wondered why they came to watch them practice. He wasn't sure he liked that idea. He knew how to play, but he wasn't the best player, and he didn't want anyone to see him goof up.

On the other hand, it might be nice having a cheering section. Especially if Bailey Winters was a part of it. This could give him the chance to impress her a little like Uncle Pete talked about.

"Okay, gang, listen up." Pastor Vink walked onto the field. "We're playing another church team tonight, all in good fun, and I've assigned each of you to a position so I can get a feel for how you play." He began to recite who went where. "Christopher Slater, you'll be playing in the outfield."

Not a very glamorous job, but he figured the older kids got the best positions. At least this way he wouldn't have to worry about messing up too much. And if he caught a fly ball, all the better.

Just then a couple more kids walked onto the field. He recognized one of them from the teen group, but he wasn't quite sure who the other one was. He was too far away. The kid had on jeans, a white shirt, and a blue ball cap. But there was something familiar about his walk. Just then he turned sideways, and Christopher spotted a ponytail coming out of the back of the kid's hat. When he walked closer, Christopher could see "the kid" was Bailey Winters! How could he impress her if she played on the team? He hadn't thought about girls being on the team. Of course, they would be. They didn't exactly live in the Dark Ages anymore. What was he thinking?

Pastor Vink called out that Bailey would be covering second base. Everyone took his or her place and the other team came up to bat. Christopher was bummed that Bailey was a ways in front of him.

She seemed pretty good at catching fly balls during the warm-up. He caught a couple himself. He hoped she noticed.

Once the bases were loaded with a new player up to bat, the pitcher threw the ball and the batter slammed the bat hard against it. A whack blasted through the air and the ball sailed straight toward Christopher. The moment seemed almost to go by in slow motion. This was it, his one chance to make good in front of Bailey. He was about to make softball history; he could feel it. His knees bent and he shoved himself up, up, up, arm extended until the ball smacked into his palm so hard, he nearly lost his balance. But he held tight as his feet came into contact with the ground.

Christopher spotted the player trying to steal second base. He could already hear the roar of victory cheers in his mind as he reared back—in perfect form, he was sure—fingers clutching the ball, and with a whoosh, released that ball with all the force of a pro, causing a ripple through the bleachers. The ball headed straight for Bailey Winters.

She would catch it, they would win the game and he and Bailey would be the heroes. The whole thing played out in his mind in a matter of seconds. He could see confetti falling from the sky, hear the deafening cheers of fans wild with applause and hear a band playing a victory tune until . . . until . . . Bailey jumped for the ball, missed it, and then crashed to the ground with a sickening thud.

The band disappeared. The confetti evaporated. The crowd —all five people in the bleachers—didn't make a peep.

Everyone hovered over Bailey.

SAM POKED HIS HEAD into Christopher's bedroom the following morning. Christopher was sitting on the edge of his bed, completely miserable.

"Hey, I hear you gave your girlfriend a busted wrist," Sam teased. "That's not exactly the way to get her to like you, you know."

"Shut up, Sam." Christopher was in no mood for his brother's teasing this morning.

He knew he had blown all possible chances with Bailey. He didn't need his brother to tell him that. The whole humiliating event replayed in his mind, over and over. He groaned.

"Hey, little bro, just kidding." Sam walked into the room and closed the door behind him. "Don't worry about it. You didn't make her jump for the ball and trip her on the way down. It's just a hazard of the game."

Christopher shrugged. Easy for Sam to say. Toby sat at his feet, trying to comfort him, but it didn't work. Nothing could cheer him up at this point.

"Shake it off, Chris. It's too bad it happened, but it wasn't your fault." Sam tousled Christopher's hair.

Christopher wished Sam would quit doing that. He wasn't a little kid anymore.

Sam hesitated and Christopher wished he'd just leave him alone. He wasn't in the mood to talk to anyone just yet this morning.

"Why don't you go see her?" Sam asked.

Christopher looked up. "Go see her? She'd probably throw things at me."

"I'm sure she wouldn't—especially if you come bearing gifts." Sam grinned.

"Gifts?"

"Yeah. Take her some flowers or get some chocolates for her, to make her feel better. I can loan you some money if you need it."

"No, I got some from Uncle Pete when I helped him in the barn a while back."

"You haven't spent that yet?"

"No. Grandpa says anything worth having is worth saving for," Christopher said, parroting his grandpa's views on money.

It looked like a frown crossed Sam's face, but it left as soon as it came.

"Well, there you go. This seems like a good time to spend a little of it."

Christopher's spirits perked up slightly. "Maybe you're right." He thought a moment. "She won't think we're like serious or anything, will she?"

Sam laughed. "I doubt it. Few girls get serious in seventh grade."

Christopher was glad of that. She was pretty and all, but he wasn't quite ready to take that step.

"But I don't even know where she lives," Christopher whined.

"No problem. We'll just call Pastor Vink and find out," Sam said.

"Okay, that's a good idea. Thanks, Sam."

"Glad to help." Sam gave him one more head tussle and walked out of the room.

Christopher pondered the conversation a little longer, and then hopped out of bed to get dressed. He'd better get those flowers before he changed his mind.

CHARLOTTE STRAIGHTENED the canisters on the kitchen counter while Sam fished for a cookie from the cookie jar. Christopher sauntered into the room.

"Sam, would you have time to take me to Filly's Flower Shop?" Christopher asked.

Sam grinned. "Sure thing."

Charlotte couldn't imagine why Christopher would need to go there.

"Thanks." He turned to Charlotte. "Okay if I go out for a little bit with Sam, Grandma?"

"Well, sure, I suppose so. What's the occasion?"

"That girl who broke her wrist last night? I thought I'd express my sympathies with flowers."

Charlotte suppressed a chuckle. "Sympathies are more for funerals, but maybe you could encourage her."

"Yeah, that's it."

Charlotte smiled. "I think that's a lovely idea." She wiped the table with a cloth, grinning at the idea of Christopher trying to impress a girl with flowers. "Now, you say this was a new girl who broke her wrist?"

"Yeah. Some welcome into the teen group I gave her, huh?" Christopher said with a pout.

"Why would you blame yourself, honey? The way I heard it, you threw the ball, she tried to catch it and fell instead. That was hardly your fault. You couldn't foresee how she would catch it."

"I guess."

"Shall I call the church and get her address?" Charlotte offered.

"Sure, that would be great, Grandma," Christopher agreed.

While Charlotte rinsed the dishcloth, Christopher headed to the family room to go on the computer.

Charlotte shook her head and smiled as she walked over to the kitchen drawer where the phone book and church directory were kept.

She pulled out the latest version of the church directory and promptly called Karen Ellis.

"Hi, Karen, this is Charlotte Stevenson. Do you have a minute?"

"Yep. What can I do to help you?"

"I was wondering if you could give me the address and phone number of Bailey Winters's family. Christopher wants to make a peace offering."

"Oh, sure. Nice family, from what I've seen. Bailey is their only child."

"I see. What are the parents' names, do you remember?"

"Craig and Dina Winters, I believe. I have their phone number right here, as a matter of fact. And their address."

"Thanks so much, Karen," Charlotte said. "See you soon."

She turned to the boys and handed Sam the paper with the Winters' address on it.

"We'll be back later this afternoon," Sam said.

"All right. Behave yourselves," Charlotte called after them. Not that it helped, but it always made her feel better to say that.

As Sam had indicated, she assumed this new girl was the reason for Christopher's lack of appetite lately. If so, her heart ached for her lovesick grandson. Of all the girls he could have thrown the ball to and then have this unfortunate accident, well, it was too bad it was the girl of his dreams.

After the boys left, Charlotte studied the piece of paper with the family's contact information on it. She had a few chores to do first, but as soon as she was done with them she'd offer a Stevenson family welcome to the new folks at church.

CHRISTOPHER STOOD at the front door of Bailey's house, staring at the doorbell as though one touch could catapult him into another time, another place. Maybe it was wishful thinking on his part.

He considered running away and forgetting the whole thing, but he heard footsteps near the door. Too late.

With the flowers clenched in his fist, he held them to his side, petals drooping toward the sidewalk, when the door opened.

"Yes, may I help you?" the woman said.

Most likely Bailey's mom. She looked like her.

"I, uh, well, uh—"

Bailey walked up behind her mom. "Christopher?"

He gulped. Out loud. They both heard him. Her mother grinned.

"This is Christopher Slater from the church youth group," Bailey said. "This is my mom."

"How nice of you to visit, Christopher," Mrs. Winters said, opening the door. "Please, come in." She looked up and spotted Sam in the car. "Is he with you?"

"Yes, ma'am," Christopher said.

"He's welcome to come in too."

"I don't think he wants to. He's messing with something on his phone."

"Sounds like fun," she said.

Christopher and Bailey stood awkwardly in the hallway.

"What are you doing here?" she asked, getting the conversation going.

"I wanted to see how you were doing, and to say I'm sorry about what happened."

"It wasn't your fault. I landed on uneven ground and couldn't hold my balance."

"Would you kids like something to drink?"

"No, thanks," Christopher said. He was thirsty but he couldn't risk spilling something just now.

"Are those for me?" Bailey asked, pointing to the upside-down flowers in his hand.

"What?" He looked down at the flowers and lifted them. "Oh, yeah. Yeah, these are for you." He passed them to Bailey. "You know, as a get-well thing."

She took a deep whiff of the bouquet. "Thanks."

His tongue felt thick against his throat, like he'd just eaten half a jar of peanut butter.

"Would you like me to put those in water for you, honey?" her mom asked.

"Sure. Thanks, Mom."

Mrs. Winters walked away with the flowers and Bailey showed Christopher into the living room. She sat on the sofa and he sat on a chair away from her.

He studied his hands. Then swallowed hard a time or two. The Winters had a mantel clock that sure ticked loudly.

"So how does your wrist feel?" he asked.

She lifted her arm with the cast. "It still hurts a lot, but I'll manage."

"I'm sorry that you can't play anymore this season."

"Yeah, I'm really bummed. I guess I'll just come and watch the games, but it won't be as much fun."

The phone rang. Christopher heard Bailey's mother answer it.

"Yeah." He felt a teensy twinge of excitement stir through him. Maybe she'd watch him play.

"You have a pretty good arm," she said.

She had noticed. He sat up taller. Maybe Uncle Pete was right. He flexed his muscles as discreetly as possible.

"Thanks," he said. "You do too." That was all right to say, wasn't it? Could he tell a girl she had a good arm?

"Well, I used to have one," she said with a laugh.

He groaned inwardly. If only he knew how to talk to girls.

"Well, just wanted to stop and give you those flowers and let you know I'm sorry about everything."

"No problem," she said. "Thanks for the flowers."

She walked him to the door.

Mrs. Winters walked into the hallway. "So nice of you to come calling, Christopher. That was your grandmother on the phone. She just invited us for Sunday dinner. Looks as though we'll be seeing you tomorrow at church and for dinner." Another broad smile.

Christopher smiled back at both of them and then walked out the door, praying all the way they couldn't hear his heart wreaking havoc in his rib cage.

He couldn't imagine getting through a whole meal with Bailey sitting at the same table. What was Grandma thinking?

꙳ Chapter Fourteen

S am followed his family out of church, and was glad he didn't have to be on the lookout for Arielle. She had already left for college. It had been awkward trying to avoid her at church since they broke up.

Some days he felt like a real loser. He took a deep breath and then let out a frustrated sigh. That was one advantage to staying in school—there were plenty of girls around. If he quit college, it would be harder to meet anyone.

Jake and Paul ran up to him, knowing they'd find him here on a Sunday morning even though they rarely attended themselves.

"Hey, Sam, where you going in such a hurry?" Jake asked.

"I'm hungry. Headed for Grandma's good grub."

"We're going over to the Harding mall, and then we can go home, change clothes and go skateboarding. Thought you might like to go with us. We'll grab some food at the mall."

Paul slapped him on the back. "It's our last day to hang out before we all head for school. Don't you start tomorrow?"

Sam nodded. "Yep."

"We leave this week too."

"Okay, I'll let my grandma know and then I'll meet up with you in the parking lot."

They discussed where they were all parked and Sam ran over to his grandma, explaining the situation.

"You don't want to eat with the family?"

"Of course I want to. But this is our last time to get together before school."

"All right," she said. "But since school starts tomorrow, I want you home for the evening meal."

"Okay." Sometimes he wished his grandma wasn't so big on family being together all the time.

"And behave yourself," she said.

"I won't do anything you wouldn't do," he said with an ornery grin and a wink.

"Oh, you. Get out of here." She waved him away with a chuckle.

Sam jumped into his car and followed the guys to Jake's house. When they got there, Jake and Paul left their cars and climbed into Sam's car so they could hang out together on the way to the mall and back.

"Dude, I noticed you got some new rags. Very preppy of you," Jake said to Sam.

"Yeah, I decided I needed some new clothes to impress the girls."

"Did you get a raise or something?" Paul asked.

"Nope. Just took Jake's advice and got a credit card." He wiggled his eyebrows.

"Oh, man, I try to stay away from those," Paul said. "I want to get rich one day, and those little cards eat up your money like nobody's business."

"Always the voice of reason," Jake said. "Let us have some fun. I, for one, don't want to think about responsibilities yet. I'll have time to make money when I'm forty. Right now, I just want to enjoy the good life."

"Me too," Sam said.

Paul shook his head. "Okay, but don't blame me when you guys are in major debt, working two jobs just to keep your heads above water, while I'm sailing on my yacht with a girl on each arm."

"Don't you wish, soldier boy," Sam said, giving him a playful slug on the shoulder.

Once they arrived at the mall, Sam pushed Paul's words far behind him and checked his wallet to make sure he had his credit card. Then he headed straight to another store.

ONCE THE TABLE was set and everyone sat down, Bob said grace over the Sunday meal. Christopher tried to swallow but couldn't. Bailey sat right across from him, and he was afraid to eat. What if something got stuck between his teeth? His stomach gurgled and he sucked it in, praying Bailey didn't hear it or if she did, she didn't know it was his stomach.

After prayer, Grandma passed the serving bowls.

"So nice of you to have us over, Charlotte. This roast looks wonderful," Mrs. Winters said.

Mr. Winters heartily agreed.

"We're so glad you could come." Grandma scooped some corn onto her plate and turned to Bailey. "How do you like the teen group, dear?"

"I like it a lot. Everyone has been so nice to me," she said, with a glance at Christopher.

He wasn't sure if it was a happy glance or a glance that said everyone else was nice to her except for Christopher. After all, he was the reason she had her wrist in a cast.

Spooning green beans onto his plate, he passed the serving bowl to Emily, who sat beside him. He glanced at Bailey's hand with the cast and watched her maneuver food onto her fork. She did pretty well, which made him feel better.

The grown-ups talked about church and the message while Christopher tried to think of how he could get away from the table without being rude.

"Christopher, I thought after the meal you could take Bailey and show her around the farm," Grandma said.

"Uh, yeah, sure," he said.

Emily gave him a discreet nudge with her elbow into his side.

He shot a glance at Bailey to make sure she hadn't seen, and then turned a frown to Emily. She just snickered.

"So Christopher, what's your favorite sport?" Bailey asked.

"Um." He swallowed hard, and then scooped some green beans onto his fork, dropping one in his lap in the process. His gaze flashed to her to see if she had noticed the mishap.

She had noticed but then had looked away while he plunked it back onto his plate. Why did he have to be so clumsy?

Emily started to laugh until she looked at him. Then she covered her mouth with her napkin. He wanted to deck her.

"I like lots of sports," he finally said.

"Me too. My dad calls me sporty."

"Does your wrist hurt today?" he asked.

"No. I'm getting used to it." She lifted her fork in demonstration. She took a bite of mashed potatoes and swallowed. She looked around. Christopher wondered if she was bored.

"Have you ever been to a farm before?" Christopher asked.

"No."

That was all she said. Didn't say she wanted to see it or anything. The ball in his stomach grew.

"It's pretty cool. There's always a lot to do."

She merely nodded but didn't say anything. He was growing more uncomfortable with every moment.

They slipped into silence while the grown-ups around them talked. He wondered if Bailey felt as miserable as he did. Maybe she hated being there. Maybe she didn't like him at all. He wasn't manly enough. That had to be why she wasn't talking. His muscles were sore from lifting those stupid weights. He didn't know how he could practice any more than he had been already.

After the meal, he and Bailey headed out to the barn.

"I never understood why barns were always painted red," Bailey said.

"I don't know. Maybe so you can see them in the winter," Christopher said with a laugh.

Bailey just kept walking without saying anything.

"I won't show you the shed. It's full of Grandpa's junk and his old rusty tractors. The shed burned down a while back, so we had to get a new one. Grandma stays clear of it so she won't get mad at Grandpa."

"My dad has a gun collection. Mom's not thrilled about those either."

"Is he a hunter?"

"Yeah."

"Cool."

"I don't think so. I hate that he kills animals."

"Oh." He wasn't sure what to say after that.

They stepped into the barn. The horses stamped and snorted. Their milk cow, Trudy, mooed and soon the others joined in.

The tart smell of horses and hay scented the air. "It sort of stinks in here," Christopher said apologetically.

"I don't care. I love animals."

They passed the saddletree. Bailey ran her hand along a hanging saddle.

"I've never ridden a horse," she said.

"Really? We could go for a ride sometime," Christopher said. "You know, when your wrist is better."

She lifted a slight smile and nodded. It was the first hint of encouragement she'd given him. She was nice enough, but Christopher wondered how he would know whether or not she was interested in him.

They walked through the barn and Bailey rubbed the horses' noses while Christopher told their names and a little about each one. Christopher took a deep breath and noticed the sky looking dark.

"Looks like it's going to pour any minute. We should head back to the house."

"Okay, I'll race you," she said.

She took off before he knew what hit him. Bailey Winters

was one of the coolest girls he'd ever met. He ran as fast as he could to catch up with her, but she still beat him.

So much for following Uncle Pete's theory. He could hardly look manly when she beat him to the porch. They both stood gulping for air.

"You beat me fair and square," he said, trying to catch his breath.

"No big deal," she offered.

"Well, let's go in and have some of my grandma's pie," Christopher said. "You won't believe how good it is."

Bailey followed him into the house. He was just as confused as ever. She was nice, but he didn't think she "liked" him.

He had to keep pumping iron. Then she'd stand up and take notice of him. He was sure of it.

SAM WAS WEARING his new khakis and cool T-shirt. Something about the new clothes gave him more confidence. He noticed some of the girls at the mall looking his way. He couldn't imagine what his grandpa had against credit cards. When he got his paycheck on Friday, he'd pay it off and everything would be cool. Maybe then he would tell his grandparents about it and prove to them he was financially responsible.

They walked into the music store, and Sam couldn't believe how different the store seemed today. Usually, he felt sort of depressed when he went in there because he could never afford to get anything, but now, he could hardly wait to look around.

"Check this out," Paul said, holding up the latest Green Day CD.

Sam and Jake gathered round him.

"I don't have that one yet," Jake said.

"Me either. I think I might get it for my car," Sam said.

"Didn't you just get a couple of tunes this week?" Jake asked.

"Yeah. What are you, the financial warden?" Sam asked, feeling a tad resentful that Jake was keeping tabs.

"Dude, you'd better watch it. Paul's right—you have to watch those credit cards or they'll get out of hand."

"Whatever," Sam said. He wasn't about to back out of getting the new tunes now. It was the principle of the thing.

"I'm telling you, Sam, you'd better be careful," Paul warned.

"What's with you guys? I'm just having a little fun. It's all within my upcoming salary. I've been setting aside money to pay for the Visa bill when it comes. Stop worrying. You're acting like my grandparents."

They went through several clothing stores, bought lunch in the food court and finally headed back to Sam's car. Once inside, Sam started the engine but it merely cranked out a weird grinding noise, shivered, and then fell silent.

Sam tried it again. Same response.

"Did you run out of gas?" Paul asked.

Sam glanced at the gauge. "No, we still have half a tank." He tried it again.

Nothing.

"We don't want to flood the engine. Let's take a look under the hood," Jake said.

The guys climbed back out and looked under the hood, though Sam suspected none of them knew much about cars.

"You gonna call your grandparents?" Jake asked.

"Oh, man, I hate to do that. They have company over for lunch. Let me think a minute."

"You could call a tow truck to take it somewhere, but that would cost plenty," Paul said.

The August heat stifled Sam. He hated the thought of sitting around waiting for help. Stupid car.

"I'll call my uncle Pete," he said, punching the numbers on his cell phone. "He'll know what to do."

When Pete answered the phone, Sam explained what was going on. They talked a minute, and then Sam clicked off his phone.

"What did he say?" Jake asked.

"He said he had to finish something but he'd be here within about an hour."

Jake groaned. "Doesn't look like we'll go skateboarding today."

"Might as well go in and grab a soda till he gets here," Paul said. Then he looked at Sam. "Guess you won't be spending your money to pay off your Visa after all."

"Thanks, Paul. I feel much better now." Sam shoved his hand in his pocket as though by some magic he'd pull out the money he needed.

He would have paid off his credit card. Could he help it that his car broke down?

Then an even worse thought hit him. His grandma would have to drive him to campus on his first day of college.

Chapter
Fifteen

Emily walked out to the barn to feed the cats. One whiff of the barn smells brought a flood of memories this morning. She remembered her first day on the farm and how foreign everything had seemed to her then. And rightfully so. She had come from San Diego, not exactly Green Acres.

"Here, kitty, kitty," she said, placing the filled food bowl on the barn floor.

The cats came running, eagerly digging into their food.

She remembered that too. How neat it was to see all the animals—well, except for the chickens. She'd never become a fan of the chickens—smelly, dirty, squawking chickens.

She walked over to the horse stalls. They watched her with interest. The smell of hay lifted as the horses stirred in their stalls. She talked to each one and ran her hand along their noses. Once she reached Stormy's stall, she unchained the gate and stepped inside.

"How are you, Stormy?" She rubbed the horse's mane and cuddled his nose while feeding him hay. Stormy was her mom's horse and sometimes just being near Stormy made Emily feel better. When she and her brothers first moved to the farm, she found great solace in staying out in the barn with the animals.

Her world had turned upside down then. Now, she sometimes forgot her life in San Diego. The farm had turned out much better than she had originally feared.

She picked up the pitchfork and freshened Stormy's stall with clean hay. How she had resented this work in the beginning. Resented her mom for dying. Resented her grandparents for making her live on this farm.

And now? Well, she still missed her mom, of course, but she was so thankful that her grandparents had willingly taken them in. Especially now that she'd gone through that babysitting course. As brief as it was, it had given her a new perspective on children and the responsibilities involved in caring for them.

Watching Will over the weekend had made her a nervous wreck. He cried practically the whole time. She checked his diaper, fed him, did everything Aunt Anna had told her to do, and nothing helped. Finally, just before Aunt Anna and the girls returned, he fell asleep.

"Well, what are you doing in here?"

Emily turned to her Grandma. "Oh, hi. Just cleaning Stormy's stall."

"What brought that on?" Grandma took a broom to the middle of the floor and set to sweeping.

"I don't know. Just thinking, I guess."

Grandma pulled the dirt into a pile, scooped it up, and threw it away in the trash bin. She turned to Emily. "About what?"

Emily shrugged. "About how hard it was to watch Will the other night." Emily couldn't believe she'd admitted that to Grandma.

"Oh?" She stepped closer to her granddaughter.

"He cried the whole time, Grandma. Till just before Aunt Anna came home. I was a mess by the time she got there."

"What did she say?"

"I didn't tell her. Didn't want her to think I wasn't up to the job. I mean, babysitting is easy, right? Why did I have so much trouble watching him?"

"Who ever said it was easy?"

"Middle school kids do it, Grandma. How hard can it be?"

"Depends on the kid, of course, but babysitting is a big job. And it's quite a responsibility."

Emily could definitely agree with that one. When she had agreed to do this job, she thought it would be a cinch. Now she wasn't so sure.

"You'll be fine, dear. Babies take some getting used to. They require lots of attention."

"How do moms do it when they have several kids?" She couldn't imagine it.

Grandma shrugged. "Somehow you manage."

"I don't think I want any kids."

Grandma laughed and pulled Emily into a hug. "Oh, you'll do fine. In fact, I think you'll be a wonderful mother. You're nurturing and careful. Your children will be lucky to have you."

"Hey, you're assuming an awful lot."

"That is, if you have children one day," Grandma added

with a wink. "Which I hope you do—wait a minute. What am I saying? That would make me a great-grandma. I don't think I'm ready for that yet." She chuckled.

Emily joined her.

"So are you babysitting this week?"

"That's the plan."

"You just need a little dose of confidence—that's all."

"Why do you think Will was crying so much?"

"Who knows? You did everything I would have done. Sometimes babies are cranky because their tummy hurts, or maybe he just missed his mommy."

"Maybe." Emily wasn't so sure.

"At any rate, I'm sure it will be better this week. Just you wait. You'll see that I'm right."

Emily smiled up at her grandma and hoped she was right. She couldn't take another three hours with a screaming baby.

SAM'S FIRST DAY OF CLASSES and here he was waiting for his grandma to pick him up in front of the library. He shouldn't complain, though. At least he had a ride. Who knew how long his car would be laid up? He spotted his grandma's car pulling into the drive and finally up to the curb. He wished he could look like anybody else. He slipped into the car and prayed Grandma would hit the accelerator. She didn't. She pulled out like, well, a grandma.

Sam sunk further into his seat and yanked his baseball cap down on his forehead.

"How was your first day?"

"It was all right," he said, trying to keep a low profile till they got off campus.

"What's the matter with you?" Grandma asked.

"Just feel sort of stupid having my grandma pick me up from college."

"Oh, I see. Well, it can't be helped till your car gets fixed. Did you call Bill and tell him you couldn't come in to work today?"

"Yeah." His stomach churned. Not only did he have to sink all his money into his car, but he now was also losing money because he couldn't get to work.

"Hopefully, the car repair place will call this afternoon, and they'll have it up and running in no time."

"Yeah."

"Listen, Sam, I know you're worried about the money, but don't borrow trouble. It may be a small matter."

He had a bad feeling about it all, but he didn't say anything. Visions of all his new stuff, along with a lengthy Visa bill flashed across his mind.

His grandma had no idea how bad things were for him. He hoped she never found out.

AFTER SHE BROUGHT Sam home, Charlotte stuffed a load of white clothes into the washing machine, added the liquid detergent, and set it to whirring. She thought about Emily's babysitting adventure and Sam's car problem. They were little problems in comparison to some folks' problems, but frustrating nonetheless. She and Hannah were scheduled to leave soon—if Hannah didn't decide to take someone else. Hopefully, nothing else would happen between now and then. She would be hard-pressed to leave if her family had any more trouble.

"Hey, Grandma?" Christopher stepped into view.

"Yes?"

He rubbed above his lip. "Do you think I should start shaving?"

She certainly hadn't seen that one coming.

"Hmm, I hadn't thought about it. Why? Do you?"

He now stroked his chin thoughtfully while Charlotte tried to contain her amusement. "I've been giving it some thought lately, thinking it might be time."

"You might want to talk to one of the guys about that, Christopher. I don't see a real need for it at present." She stepped closer to look at his upper lip. Try as she might, she could barely make out the baby fuzz.

He searched her face as though anticipating the possibilities.

She hated to burst his bubble. "I know you're in a hurry to grow up, but once you start shaving, you never get a break. If I were you, I'd hold off as long as possible."

Before Christopher could comment, Bob slammed the door as he stepped through the back door into the kitchen.

"I'm telling you, if I were a swearing man . . ." He yanked off his shoes.

Christopher muttered, "That can't be good," and darted out of the room.

"Bob, what is it?" Charlotte had never heard him talk like that.

"Charlotte, I've had about all I can take of Andy Weber. He's like a good man gone bad with power."

The very idea of fragile, wiry Andy Weber as power mad made her chuckle—until Bob turned a glare her way.

"I'm sorry, Bob, but you have to admit that's quite a picture you've conjured up there. Andy is hardly the power-driven type."

"That's what I thought too, before I started working for him." Bob sat at the table and Charlotte poured him some coffee, their afternoon routine.

"Well, fortunately, it will all be over soon."

"Not soon enough for me. I'm trying to keep our friendship ever before me, but it's on a thin rope, I can tell you that."

Just then the phone rang. Charlotte put the coffee carafe back on the counter and walked over to answer it. "Hello?"

"Hi, Charlotte. This is Brad Weber. Is Bob home yet?"

"He sure is. Hang on just a second."

Bob looked at her.

"It's Brad Weber."

Bob frowned. "Hello? Yeah. Yeah. Okay. Can't be helped. Be safe. Bye."

"Family member sick and in the hospital," he said. "They're not coming home this weekend after all. They're staying an extra week. I'll have to cover until a week from this Friday." Bob locked eyes with Charlotte. "I'm not happy about this."

"OKAY IF I JOIN YOU?" Emily asked Sam when she approached him on the porch swing that evening.

"Free country," he said.

She eased onto the wooden swing. "It sure is hot out here."

"Yeah."

"How was your first day of college?"

He glared at her. "How do you think it was? It's school. How good can it be?"

Her eyebrows raised. She hadn't expected that reaction. "I thought you were looking forward to college."

"Would you, if you were still living with your grandparents?"

"I see your point."

"Not only that but Grandma had to drop me off and pick me up."

Emily groaned in sympathy.

"Some of my friends went straight to working and they're having an awesome time of it. Others left home and they're partying at school. Me? It's just like high school."

"Yeah, but at least you won't have their debt when you get out."

"Why does everybody say that? What's the big deal? Everyone has debt. You have debt when you buy a car, a house, have a kid. Everything takes money." His voice was tight.

"Whoa. What's the matter with you?"

Sam ran his hand through his hair and let out a sigh. "Sorry, sis. I'm just upset."

"Anything I can help you with?" Emily asked.

He leaned in to her. "Can you keep a secret?"

"Sure, I can."

"I did something really stupid. I applied for, and got, a Visa."

Her eyes widened. How many times had Grandpa spoken of the dangers of credit card use?

"Yeah, I know. As I said, stupid. But my plan was to pay it off when I got the bill. All of it."

"That's not such a bad plan."

He studied the calluses on his fingers. "That was before my car broke down."

"Oh."

"Just found out it's gonna cost me a hunk of change. No way I can pay off the credit card now. At the rate of interest they charge on that card, it will take me forever to catch up."

"I'm sorry, Sam."

"Yeah, me too. I have to have a car so there's no way around this. The car comes first. I hadn't even thought about something happening to prevent me from paying that stupid bill."

"Worst-case scenario, Grandpa calls it."

"He would blow a gasket if he knew what I'd done."

"Best to keep it to yourself," she agreed. "No use stirring up more trouble. Besides, he's got enough on his mind just dealing with working at the store and helping Mr. Weber."

"You're right," Sam said.

Silence hovered between them.

"Sam, you remember when you worked at the day care and that kid went missing?"

"How could I ever forget it? At least the money problem isn't as bad as that nightmare."

"Yeah," she said. "I was just wondering about that."

"Why?"

"I guess because I'm babysitting and stuff."

"Oh." He nodded.

"It's hard work to watch kids."

"It sure is. Scares me to death," he said. "I don't think I'll ever do it again."

"I had no idea, you know, when I took this job for Aunt Anna," Emily said, running her fingers along the chain on the swing.

"I imagine Aunt Anna isn't exactly the easiest person to work for either."

"Some days she's harder to please than others. And after that babysitting class and all, well, it just made me see what a responsibility kids are."

"You got that right. Makes you want to think long and hard before you have kids of your own. They cost a lot of money too."

"I suppose."

"Don't worry about it, Emily. I'm sure you do a fine job of watching Will."

"He cries a lot," she admitted.

"That would drive me crazy." He stretched his legs.

"It's pretty upsetting. Especially when nothing I do seems to help."

"You're talking to the wrong person, if you think I have any words of wisdom about kids. I'm clueless."

"I'm beginning to think I am too."

The creaking swing moved back and forth, back and forth.

"Thanks for talking, Sam. Don't worry about school. I think in the long run, you'll be glad you stayed home and saved money."

He shrugged.

She walked into the house and left him to his thoughts. She sure hoped Sam could figure out a way to get out of debt—before Grandpa found out.

⌣ Chapter
Sixteen

The next afternoon, Charlotte brought the laundry basket of whites to the family room and began folding the clothes. She could still smell the lemon spray she had used to dust earlier that morning. She welcomed September's arrival with open arms and could hardly wait for it to arrive this year. August heat forced her to keep the air-conditioning on and the windows closed most of the time. Charlotte was an open-window kind of gal. She loved the country breeze flowing through her home.

Picking up one of Bob's T-shirts, she began to fold it.

"Hi, Grandma." Emily walked into the room.

"Hi. You don't have to work for Anna today, right?"

"Right. I go over there tomorrow."

Emily plopped down and started helping Charlotte fold the clothes. "So what's going on with Hannah?"

Charlotte looked up. "What do you mean?"

Emily shrugged. "I was walking down by the Carters' place and saw Mrs. Cunningham and Mrs. Richmond over at her house. They were all getting into Mrs. Richmond's car."

"Janie Richmond from church?"

"Yeah."

Another pang of jealousy surged through Charlotte. "I don't know. Maybe they're all working on planning the church picnic." Maybe Allison was trying to edge her way into the trip. That would be just like her.

Janie and Hannah were friends. Had been for quite some time. Charlotte was fine with that. It was good to have many friends. But the idea of someone else taking her spot on the weekend getaway bothered her big time.

"Yeah, I guess so. Haven't seen her around for a few days. You two all right?"

"We're fine. Why would you ask that?"

"I don't know. I just haven't heard you on the phone with her or seen her around as much as usual. That's all. You're still going on your little trip, right?"

"Yes." This conversation irritated Charlotte, but she tried not to show it. The whole thing with Hannah was driving her to distraction.

"Good. I would hate for you to miss it. You're such good friends, and I know it will be good for you." Emily finished folding a shirt just as the phone rang. She jumped up. "That will be Ashley, I'd better get it."

She ran out of the room, but her words lingered with Charlotte. "You're such good friends . . . ."

Charlotte hoped her granddaughter was right. She would hate to lose Hannah's friendship after all these years. It was silly to think that way, of course. Hannah wouldn't toss her aside now, not after all they'd been through together.

Would she?

AFTER TAKING A BATH and putting on her pajamas, Emily went into her room and crawled into bed. She thought over her recent talk with Sam. She hated to see him so upset about money and school. Adult stuff. They were all growing up. Though she knew it was coming some day, she hated the thought of them slowly moving away, one by one.

People try to say that change is good, but she couldn't see it. The biggest change in her life came when her mom died. There had been nothing good about that.

Now they were growing up. Sure, growing up was good, she supposed. But everyone moving away, forgetting one another? No matter what anyone said, she knew that was what happened. Look at her mom. Left home and never talked to her parents. Emily didn't want to do that. She wanted to stay in touch with Grandma and Grandpa, but would she? Would they stay in touch?

Look at their dad. He hardly came around. His appearance at Christmas hadn't exactly made everything all right. She hoped she would have more of a relationship with her own kids someday—if she had any.

The rambling thoughts saddened her. She sighed. It seemed as though nothing ever stayed the same. One day she'd most likely be married, probably never get to see Ashley. As much as she thought that surely wouldn't happen, she knew it was true. She hardly talked to her best friends from San Diego anymore.

Life goes on.

Her thoughts ran back to Sam and his money problem. Maybe she could help him. She'd been working for jeans money, and she didn't have a lot of money, but it was enough to help bring down Sam's balance. She could make things a little easier for him if she offered her money.

The more she thought about it, the more she felt it was the right thing to do. She got out of bed and went over to her drawer to count her money.

She grabbed the bundle and walked to Sam's room and knocked on the door. "Sam? Can I come in?" she asked.

"Yeah, it's open."

She walked into his room. "Listen, I know it's not enough to cover everything, but, well, I've been saving some money, and here, I want you to have it." She threw her small bundle on his bed.

His jaw dropped. "I thought you were saving for school clothes."

She shrugged. "I have enough."

He picked up the bundle and went over to give her a brotherly hug. "You're pretty cool, you know that?"

"So I've been told once or twice."

He stepped back and looked at her, arms on her shoulders. "But here's the deal. I got myself into this mess, and I'm going to get myself out. I'm going to see if Uncle Bill will let me put in some extra hours. I'll get this paid off. But your offer, that's really something, sis. I won't forget it. But I won't take it either." He reached over and hugged her once more.

"Thanks," he whispered.

"You're welcome."

He stuffed the money into her hand and she slipped back out the door, just as Grandma was walking down the hallway.

She sure hoped Grandma hadn't overheard anything.

"HERE ARE YOUR CLOTHES, SAM," Charlotte said, dropping the basket of folded laundry on his floor.

"Thanks, Grandma." His gaze was glued to a textbook page. He didn't look up.

Charlotte slipped out of the bedroom and down the hall. She had never been one to eavesdrop, but she couldn't help overhearing Emily offer Sam money. What could be so important that Emily was willing to offer the money she'd been saving for jeans? She couldn't have a lot of money saved yet, but she offered it nevertheless.

Something was going on, no doubt about it. No one ever said part of parenting included detective work, but she'd certainly gotten her fair share of it in the past couple of years.

She smiled and eased down the stairs. They had come so far in these few years. Hard to believe the kids had been with them that long already. And that Denise had been gone that long. It still seemed so surreal, as though Denise still wasn't talking to them, but that they could contact her if they really needed her.

If only things had been different. But then that was water under the bridge. It did no good to dwell on what she could never change.

That's why she tried so hard with the grandchildren. She didn't want to make the same mistakes with them that she obviously had made with Denise.

If only she knew exactly what it was she had done wrong. The familiar ache, though less intense than it used to be, seized her heart. She attempted to shake it off as she entered the kitchen to plan tomorrow's dinner.

After Denise's death, there had been days when putting one foot in front of the other made it a good day—when all her effort went toward breathing. But life went on, and they had learned how to cope with knowing that their daughter would never come visit again.

And yet Charlotte saw her daughter almost every single day through the grandchildren—a smile, an expression, an attitude. They were reflections of Denise. The Denise they had loved and cuddled and, eventually, let go.

The tangled thoughts webbed their way back to Sam and Emily. They were growing up too fast. Way too fast.

One day soon, she would be letting them go too.

AFTER DINNER THE NEXT DAY, Charlotte and Bob settled in front of the television. Bob turned on a rerun of *The Waltons* while Christopher and Emily played checkers on a corner table. Charlotte worked on embroidering a towel for a friend at church. The smell of the buttered popcorn they had eaten earlier still lingered in the air.

"Where's Sam?" Emily asked.

"He's working late at Bill's office tonight," Charlotte said.

"Why's he doing that?" Bob wanted to know.

"They needed him, I guess," Charlotte said, poking her needle into the fabric and sliding the thread through.

A makeup commercial filled the TV screen and Christopher looked up from his checker game. "What is that?" he asked, nodding toward the TV.

"The eyebrow pencil and liner?" Emily asked.

"Yeah."

She rolled her eyes. "It's what women use on their eyes, doofus."

"Why?"

"To make them look pretty."

He turned and watched the commercial as the model used the pencil on her eyebrows, feathering with small strokes, filling in the empty places. He shook his head.

"King me," Emily said.

Christopher looked back to the checkerboard and frowned. "Hey. How did you do that? Did you cheat when I wasn't looking?"

Emily looked totally offended. "I did not cheat. That's what you get for not paying attention."

Looking none too happy, Christopher picked up a checker and topped her man with it.

Charlotte tried not to chuckle. He never ceased to amuse her. She wondered what his interest in the makeup commercial was about.

"I won," Emily shouted with far too much glee in her voice.

"I'm done." Christopher had a scowl on his face as he got up.

"Spoilsport," Emily said.

He started to walk away.

"Hey, you have to help me put this away."

He walked back to her and helped put the checkers back in the box.

"I'm going up to my room, Grandma," Christopher said.

"All right, honey."

"Can I call Ashley?" Emily asked.

"Sure. How has she been?" Charlotte asked.

"She's been fine. Working a lot for her mom so she can make extra money."

"Oh, that's right," Charlotte said, tucking an end piece of green thread under a red thread.

Emily went into the other room to call her friend and Charlotte's thoughts went to Melody Givens, Ashley's mom. Melody had been diagnosed with breast cancer earlier in the year, and Charlotte was so thankful her friend had seemingly healed nicely from the whole trauma. It had been quite an ordeal for the family and for the community. But the community had stood by Mel, and her business not only survived—it had thrived during the trial.

She watched the kids leave the room. Yes, she believed with family and friends, one could face just about anything.

Even teenagers.

CHRISTOPHER SPOTTED the eyeliner on the bathroom counter. He knew it belonged to Emily. He quickly closed the bathroom door, grabbed the pencil, and looked into the mirror. He used short "feathery" strokes, like the announcer on the radio said, on his upper lip to see if it could pass for a mustache.

It couldn't.

He had figured as much, but was desperate to get Bailey to notice him. He watched how she looked at the older boys, and he didn't see her looking at him that way.

With a sigh, he grabbed a dark washcloth and scrubbed off the eyeliner. Back to the drawing board.

When he left the bathroom, he noticed that Sam's door was open. He wasn't home yet, so Christopher tiptoed into his brother's bedroom. He thought Sam had mentioned buying some cologne recently but as he glanced around the room he didn't see anything. Uncle Pete had said something about cologne too. Maybe he needed to buy some. Yes, that's what he would do.

Surely Bailey would notice him then.

Chapter
Seventeen

W ant to go in here? Maybe we can get a soda," Christopher said to Dylan when they parked their bikes in front of Kepler's Pharmacy the next afternoon.

"Sure. I'm hot."

Christopher saw only a few customers when they stepped inside the store. One elderly woman talked to Mr. Kepler, while Nora, the photo clerk, worked on something at the counter.

"Hello, boys," Mr. Kepler said when they entered. The rosy color of his cheeks enhanced the cheery look of the old man, while a smile lit his blue eyes.

"Hi, Mr. Kepler."

The pharmacist turned his attention back to his customer. Dylan stopped to look at a comic on display while Christopher eavesdropped on the customer and the lady at the makeup counter. He'd never seen her before.

"This one is especially popular with men." She sprayed a little on the cuff of the woman's shirt and the woman smiled. "Oh, that is nice. Okay, I'll get it. I just wanted something different this year for his birthday. I hardly ever buy him cologne."

Dylan stuffed the magazine back in the rack before Christopher could get a glimpse of the cologne the woman was talking about. He had to find out. It could be just the thing he needed to get Bailey's attention.

Still, he couldn't risk it with Dylan around. They picked up a can of soda pop each and paid for them. Just as they got outside and walked up to their bikes, Christopher announced that he wanted to get a pack of gum and he'd be right back.

He darted back into the pharmacy in hopes of asking that lady at the counter about the cologne. She wasn't there. In fact, there was no help in sight, except for Mr. Kepler who was figuring something with a pencil at the register. Christopher hoped Mr. Kepler didn't see him looking at the colognes. Christopher didn't want him to make a big deal of it just in case Dylan walked back in.

Leaning in, Christopher searched the counter for what could be the right cologne. Most of them were in the show-case below the register. He then spotted one left on the counter.

He picked it up to check out the name, when a voice called behind him.

"Hey, Christopher. What are you doing here?"

The mere sound of Bailey Winters's voice made his fingers trigger-happy. When he turned around to greet her, he spritzed her with the scent of sweet perfume. Flowery perfume. It made them both cough. A lot.

"Oh, sorry, Bailey. Gotta go." With that, he ran out of the pharmacy as fast as he could, the girlie aroma chasing him every step of the way.

Dylan's nose crinkled up. "You smell funny."

"Come on, let's go!" Christopher had never pedaled so fast in all his life. His heart rate ramped up a notch or two. Or three. At this rate, he'd need a pacemaker before he got home.

One thing he knew for sure—this time, he had gotten Bailey's attention.

WHILE THE KIDS HOLED UP in their rooms, enjoying their privacy, Charlotte and Bob snatched a moment for themselves out on the front-porch swing, surrounded by the quiet hum of night sounds.

"That apple caramel pie tonight hit the spot," Bob said, patting his stomach. "Was there any left?"

Charlotte's eyebrows shot upward. "Do you think you should have any more? It's not a sugar-free pie. You have to be careful."

"I've been good this week. I think I can handle it."

Charlotte paused. "Let's think about that one for a bit." She hoped a little time away from the thought would make him forget about it.

"Well, if you plan to make apple pies for the church picnic on Saturday, you'd better bake an extra one for me."

She chuckled. "I'll keep that in mind."

They heard Toby's muffled bark and scuffling about coming from Christopher's room.

"Sounds like Toby and Christopher are having fun. I hope he doesn't let that dog break anything," Charlotte said.

"Oh, they'll be all right," Bob said. "They're good for each other."

Charlotte shrugged. "Things getting any better at the supply store?"

"I'd rather not talk about that. Let's talk about your trip."

She recognized that tone of voice and knew he meant business, so she let the matter drop. For now.

"I'm not so sure I want to talk about that," she said with a forced laugh.

"What do you mean by that? Aren't you looking forward to the time away with Hannah?"

"I was but now I don't know."

"Why not? You and Hannah have been the best of friends for years."

A lump rose in her throat. "I know," she whispered.

"What is it, Charlotte?"

She didn't really want to talk to Bob about it. She loved him dearly, but he wasn't great at understanding the ways of women. Besides, if she voiced her feelings it would just sound stupid.

"Oh, I don't know. Allison Cunningham made a comment that got me a little riled, I suppose. Nothing major."

He chuckled. "You know how Allison Cunningham is. You just have to consider the source."

Now Charlotte chuckled. She rarely heard Bob say anything like that.

"You and Hannah are far too close to allow someone like that to come between you. I suspect some of your concern stems from our family too. I want you to go and have a good time. We'll miss you but we'll be just fine here." With his arm around her, he gave her a light squeeze.

"Yeah, I'm sure you're right."

"And if you're having a little misunderstanding, this getaway could be just the ticket to strengthen your friendship."

She hadn't thought of that. The idea made her feel better. She turned to him and smiled. "Thanks, honey."

He smiled too. "You're welcome." The swing squeaked back and forth a couple of times and then he whispered to her, "Does that earn me an extra piece of apple pie?"

THOUGH CHRISTOPHER had scrubbed away any trace of girlie perfume the minute he got home from Kepler's Pharmacy, he took a long shower that night to be extra certain the smell was gone for good.

Once he changed into his pajamas, he felt a lot better. He tumbled around the bedroom with Toby and after Toby tired out, the pooch settled at the foot of Christopher's bed while Christopher picked up the weights Sam had let him borrow and began his repetitions. After he finished, he got up and walked over to the mirror. He flexed his biceps. One glance told him that at this rate, he would be out of college before his muscles were big enough to notice.

Uncle Pete said girls liked older men. Did Bailey like older guys? Maybe she would like him more if he could make himself appear older.

He was about to give up in despair when an idea came to him.

BOB FINISHED WATCHING an old movie on television, and Charlotte made her way to bed. The vitamins were starting to kick in and help some, but it had been a long day and she was tired.

She knelt down by her bed. "Lord, You know what's going on with Hannah and me. I know I shouldn't listen to others. I'm not sure why Hannah seems to be avoiding me, but she may just be busy. I don't know. Whatever this struggle is between us, help us to sort through it all and may our friendship be stronger for it. Thank You for Hannah and Frank and help me to be the friend she needs. Show me how to do my part to fix this problem. Amen."

Once Charlotte rose from her knees and climbed into bed, she felt better about the situation. In fact, she decided that after breakfast in the morning, she'd go over to Hannah's for coffee and talk it out.

Yes, they would get things settled once and for all.

∿ Chapter
Eighteen

Once everyone was fed and out the door to their various destinations, Charlotte made her way to Hannah's house. Coffee cup in hand, she thought she'd just surprise her friend with a visit. They liked to do that with one another. Hannah usually came to Charlotte's but hadn't been there in a couple of days. When Charlotte mentioned it at church, Hannah had said she'd been very busy. But she didn't stand around and chat as usual, either. Something was definitely wrong.

The morning sun radiated the usual August warmth as Charlotte trudged over to Hannah's home. Birdsong whistled and chirped from a telephone wire while a lone squirrel shimmied up a tree. Charlotte spotted a car in Hannah's driveway, but couldn't place it. For a moment she wavered on whether to proceed to Hannah's or go back home. Remembering her prayer, she forced herself forward. So what if she couldn't stay. At least she'd made the effort.

She knocked on the door and mustered the best smile possible. She could hear Hannah talking to someone as her footsteps came closer to the door. It opened.

"Charlotte," she said with surprise. "Hi." She smiled but she didn't open the door until she spotted the mug in Charlotte's hand and evidently realized what was on her mind. "Come in."

Charlotte stepped inside. "I don't want to intrude. I just thought if you weren't busy, we could have coffee together."

The sweet scents of chocolate, sugar, and spices meandered through the room letting Charlotte know she'd interrupted Hannah's baking.

Just then Janie Richmond stepped into view from the kitchen. She wiped her hands on a checkered towel. "Hello, Charlotte."

Charlotte could feel her face grow warm. She was intruding. An awkward moment followed. "Hi, Janie."

"I hear you *might* take a trip with Hannah," Janie said with a smile.

Might? Did she say "might"?

"Yeah," was all Charlotte could muster.

"Sounds like a really fun weekend," Janie said.

Without skipping a beat, Hannah said, "We were just baking desserts for the church picnic tomorrow. Are you going?"

The question caught Charlotte off-guard. "Well, of course I'm going." Why would Hannah even ask such a question?

Hannah nodded but said nothing.

There was another awkward moment.

"Well, I can see you're busy. We'll do coffee another time."

"Sure, sounds good," Hannah agreed. "Thanks for stopping by. We'll see you at the picnic."

"Bye, Charlotte. Good to see you," Janie called out.

Charlotte took her mug and her battered pride and headed for home.

ONCE CHARLOTTE RETURNED from Bedford Gardens later that afternoon, she was so tired she wondered how she'd get her pies baked in time for the church picnic tomorrow. Too bad Hannah hadn't invited her over—she might have gotten her pies done too.

Climbing out of her car, she glanced at the low-hanging clouds with shades of charcoal. The air had turned cooler last evening, so she'd turned off the air-conditioning and opened some windows to air out the house. She loved the smell of fresh country air.

Another glance at the sky told her she'd have to lower the windows so the rain couldn't get inside.

Once inside the house, she sorted through the mail, placing the farm bills on the desk to deal with later. Then she dropped her purse on the desk.

Her legs ached as she made her way to the kitchen to make sure her cupboards held the items she needed to start baking. With this ordeal between her and Hannah, Charlotte's heart felt as heavy as her steps. The more she thought about it, the more she realized she did need the weekend getaway. Either she was getting older or life was getting more demanding—or maybe both. At any rate, it looked like a time of respite was in order.

Unfortunately, maybe she was getting so old that Hannah was reconsidering her as a guest. Probably wished she had asked someone else altogether.

A low growl of thunder sounded from the skies reminding her to close the windows. She shook her head and made her rounds in the kitchen and family room.

Bob had left the paper strewn across his chair. With a sigh, she bent over and picked it up, folded it, and placed it on his seat.

A woman's work was never done.

With Bob working at the store, Sam at school, Emily babysitting and Christopher at Dylan's, the house was unusually quiet. She wasn't sure she liked it. Since the kids hd moved in, the home's atmosphere had changed dramatically; noise, clutter, phone calls. She smiled with the thought. She had grown quite comfortable having the kids around. It reminded her of days gone by when her own children had been living at home. All too soon that had ended.

And all too soon they would experience an empty nest again.

Once back in the kitchen, she turned on the oven to preheat and pulled flour from the cupboard and her rolling pin and measuring cup from the drawer. She set to work mixing the dry ingredients for her piecrust on the counter.

The rain pelted the house, making smears across the windowpanes. The old homestead groaned beneath the crush of it. But it was a sturdy house. They didn't make them like this anymore. It was built of strong, heavy wood; they had taken no shortcuts when they made this place so many years ago. It was stable, durable. The Stevenson homestead was sturdy—just like the family. They'd weathered life's storms and come through—a bit battered and worn but still standing.

As she cut the shortening into the flour mixture, she thought of their new life since the grandkids had moved in. They'd had their share of struggles—what family didn't? But they'd gotten through each one. They were all learning to stretch and grow—together. As a family.

Sam seemed to be settling in to school, for which she was thankful. They had enough to think about without worrying about him staying in school. Education was so crucial these days.

As she rolled out the pie dough, Charlotte's thoughts drifted to Hannah. How many pies had they baked together over the years? Certainly enough to keep the citizens of Bedford plump and happy.

Hannah always had a new recipe for this or that pie. Charlotte liked to stay with the tried and true. Set in her ways, she supposed. That must be what age did to a person. She wouldn't blame Hannah if she asked someone younger to go on the trip.

Charlotte laid the crusts over two pie plates and formed them to the plates. She chuckled when she remembered the soggy crusts, the burned crusts, the failed meringues she and Hannah had whipped up together. The laughter, the cleanup, the . . . friendship.

The more Charlotte thought about it, the madder she got. How could Hannah throw it all away merely because Charlotte wasn't sure about going on the trip? Couldn't she understand that Charlotte hadn't been feeling well? What kind of compassion was that? Hannah was being purely selfish—that was all. Selfish.

Well, let her go on that trip with Janie or Allison or

whomever she wanted. It wouldn't bother Charlotte in the least. No matter what their ages, Charlotte felt sure she could hold her own with the best of them.

She was tired of blaming herself for everything. Hannah could have offered more understanding. She knew that Charlotte had been under extra pressure of late, what with the canning season upon her, getting the kids ready for school—who wouldn't be tired? She dumped the cherry-berry pie filling into the crust with such gusto that she splattered some of the red sauce and had to clean it up.

Charlotte topped the cherry-berry pie with another crust, crimped the edges, and cut decorative slits on top. She then shoved it into the oven, and set the timer. She'd go to that picnic with her head held high and if Allison Cunningham so much as whispered a shred of gossip ... Charlotte thought of the apple caramel pie yet to be made, rolled up her sleeves and set to work with a vengeance.

THE DEBT THING hung over Sam like a heavy rain cloud. He'd get through it, but he hoped he could do it without his grandpa knowing. The thing was, Sam didn't know when to expect the credit card bill. And he pretty much figured his grandpa knew a credit card bill when he saw one. If Grandpa got to the mail first, Sam was in trouble. Big trouble.

His boots tromped the grass as he cut across the lawn and headed toward the English Department building. He hated reading dead people's stories. Evidently, that's what they considered education.

The humidity was relentless today. He was thankful his car had air conditioning. Sam studied the sky. Clouds hung low and dark. Rain appeared imminent. He was glad he had his car back so he wouldn't have to wait in the rain for his grandma. The car repairs had been minimal. Still, he wouldn't be able to pay off his credit card ar the end of the month as originally planned. He would do it eventually, of course. He just needed to be patient.

Sam pulled the backpack off his back and slung it across his shoulder. He'd be glad to dump it when he got to class. The weight of carrying it intensified the heat.

He glanced around as he stepped onto the sidewalk. The campus was nice. They'd recently added a couple of new buildings and a huge decorative clock in the middle of the campus lawn. It was quite impressive, really.

Though he envied Jake and Paul for getting to leave home, he was glad he didn't have the expense. On the other hand, if everything was paid for . . .

"Hi. You're in my English-lit class, aren't you?" The brown-haired girl with dark eyes and long, thick lashes stepped up to him. She lifted a friendly smile and his stomach leaped with the possibilities.

"Yeah, I think so." Who was he kidding? He'd spotted her the first day of classes.

"I'm Katie Kensington."

"Sam Slater."

They shared a smile and continued walking. "So what do you think of Professor Reyes?" she asked.

"He's cool, I guess," Sam said. "I'm just not a huge fan of English lit." As soon as he said it, he wondered if he should have kept his mouth shut. After all, this might be her favorite subject.

"Yeah, me neither. I'd prefer art any day."

His kind of gal.

"So what's your major?" she asked, with eyes that held true interest.

"Don't know yet. General ed so far. Trying to find my way, you know?" He shrugged.

"I've known forever I want to be an art teacher."

Her and Arielle. Must be a girl thing.

"You'll figure it out," she said.

Something about that depressed him a little.

"Hey, I'm headed over to the coffee shop after class. Want to go?" she asked.

There was that leap again. "Sure."

She grinned. "Okay. See you then." She waved at a friend and headed over to her, blending in with the other classmates.

Sam didn't have any cash on him. He'd look like a real loser if he didn't get anything. Then he remembered.

He had his credit card.

Chapter
Nineteen

Gravel bit into the tires of the Stevenson family car as it neared the church. The roads less traveled in the Bedford countryside were a bit primitive.

"Where were you just before we left this morning, Christopher?" Charlotte asked, turning to Christopher in the back seat. "I called and called for you."

"I told Uncle Pete I was going over to the garage sale down the road. Didn't he tell you?"

"No," she said. "I suppose he was too busy finishing up in the barn before the picnic."

"I keep telling you those garage sale finds can add up. You'd better watch your money," Bob said.

"Yes, Grandpa."

Bob pulled the car up to the church and parked. Family members spilled onto the parking lot.

Bob leaned in to Charlotte. "Looks like Andy Weber made it today. Wonder if he'll try to boss me around here too."

"Now you behave yourself. We're here to have fun." Charlotte gave him a warning glance and wobbled slightly on the uneven earth and grassy lawn beneath her feet while she carried the chicken and noodles toward a table. Bob and the kids grabbed dishes of green bean casse-role, garlic mashed potatoes, and the pie, and then plunked them on the tables before scurrying off in a flash.

A polished blue sky bright with the blaze of sunlight sparkled overhead. Birds chirped in nearby trees that dotted the lawn. Charlotte felt more kick in her heels than she had in days. Women buzzed around the tables like bees around a hive, spreading an array of dishes smorgasbord-style.

Charlotte spotted Hannah working at the table where she was headed. Hannah looked up, glanced at her briefly, and then headed in the opposite direction, stopping in front of Janie Richmond.

Charlotte's next glance landed on Allison Cunningham, of all people. And wouldn't you know, Allison was looking at her too. She lifted a smirk as though she had seen the whole thing with Hannah.

Charlotte swallowed hard. That was just fine with her. Hannah could talk to whomever she wanted.

Lydia Middleton hobbled over to Charlotte. "Well, you look spiffy today, Charlotte."

"As do you, Lydia." Charlotte reached over and hugged the older woman. "You know how I love church socials." Charlotte gazed out toward the field where kids huddled in clusters, young boys chased after girls, and teenagers had already started a volleyball game. She watched Emily hit the ball and marveled how she looked more and more like Denise every day.

Lydia followed her gaze. "Oh, to be young again." She tsked and then shook her head.

Did everyone in the county think Charlotte was old? Did she need a facelift? Botox? What?

The pastor called the little community to prayer. Once the prayer was said, the lawn came alive with chatter and activity. Family breaking bread together.

Another glance at Hannah, who still stood close to Janie. She and Hannah were acting like warring siblings.

"Is that my cherry-berry pie?" Charlotte asked Bob while they sat eating at the table.

He flashed a grin. "Sure is. Can't wait to dig into it."

Charlotte tried to keep her pride at a minimum but if there was one thing that could cause her head to swell, it was her pies. She and Hannah both were known throughout Bedford for their pies and desserts.

She wondered what Hannah and Janie had made for dessert. So she could stay away from it. She knew her thoughts were bad right now—borderline un-Christian as a matter of fact—but she just couldn't seem to help herself.

She glanced across the tables and saw Hannah and Frank slide in beside Janie and her husband, Hank. A stab of pain constricted Charlotte's chest. They both had other friends, but this seemed . . . different somehow. The feeling of losing a lifetime friend was almost tangible.

"Mind if we sit here?" Melody Givens stood across the table with her husband, Russ.

"Sure, the more the merrier," Charlotte said.

They settled into their seats.

"So how are things going at the store, Bob?" Russ asked.

This couldn't be good.

"They're going great. Couldn't ask for a better helper." Andy Weber slipped into the seat beside Russ, across from Bob, surprising them.

They all stared at him.

He chuckled. "You all look like the cat who swallowed the canary. Can't I say Bob's a good worker?"

"You can indeed," Charlotte said with a smile and quick exchange of glances with her husband—whose jaw was dangling.

"He'd have to be a good worker to put up with my grousing all day."

Charlotte wanted to say amen to that but thought better of it.

His wife, Arlene, settled beside him on the seat.

"Now, Arlene, don't you say a word."

She grinned. "Wasn't going to." She situated her napkin on her lap and picked up her fork. "But I came into the store the other day and heard Andy grumping at Bob, spouting orders here and there, and I gave him what for when he came home."

Andy's expression, full of surrender, said it all. He nodded. "That she did." He looked at Bob. "Sorry if I've been a tad bossy lately, Bob."

"They changed his meds," Arlene said by way of explanation. "His personality changed along with it. Now they're trying him on something new. Sorry you got the brunt of it, Bob."

Bob just sat there speechless. Until everyone looked at him. "No problem at all, Andy. I'm sure it's not easy living with Parkinson's."

Charlotte knew Bob must have been feeling pretty horrible right about now. But at the same time, Andy's bossiness hadn't been easy on him.

"You've got that right, but I'm getting along all right. Sure don't mean to hurt my friends, though."

"No harm done," Bob said, a soft, warm look in his eyes.

"So you'll hang in there with me till Brad gets back?" Andy's eyes sparkled with hope.

"Sure will."

It seemed as if the tension at the table just lifted with the afternoon breeze. Charlotte thought about Hannah. This was what church family picnics were all about. Clearing the air. Healing. Encouraging. Strengthening friendships.

Charlotte looked toward Hannah and Janie. They were laughing together. Charlotte's head hurt just thinking about everything. She couldn't deal with it today.

She turned her attention to the kids. "It seems Christopher and Bailey have sure hit it off," she said, watching Bailey talking to him. Charlotte wasn't sure how she felt about that. They were quite young. She hoped it didn't develop into anything to worry about.

"Are you sure about that?" Bob said. "Looks to me like she's doing all the talking and Christopher would rather play ball."

Charlotte squinted and focused a little better. Now that Bob said that, she thought he just might be onto something there.

CHRISTOPHER COULDN'T believe his good fortune. Bailey was actually paying attention to him today. Maybe she did like him. Maybe his muscles were getting bigger from pumping those weights.

"Hey, will you push me on the tire swing?" she asked, hope sparkling in her eyes.

"Uh—" Christopher gulped. Right out loud. "Can you

swing with that on your hand?" he asked, pointing to the cast on her wrist, hoping that could be a deterrent.

"Of course. My fingers are free to curl around the rope. Come on, silly. Race you to the tree." She took off before he got out of his seat.

He liked her, but pushing her on the tree swing where everybody could see them?

"HEY, YOU BETTER WATCH that brother of yours," Troy said to Emily as they talked under the strong shade of a nearby tree.

"Why is that?"

He shrugged. "Just that Tommy Krinn saw him trying on girls' perfume at the pharmacy the other day."

Her gaze cut to him. "What? Is this a joke?" She made a face. The very idea was ridiculous.

"No." He held up his hand in pledge. "Scout's honor. That's what he said."

"Well, that's stupid. Why would Christopher do that?"

"That's why I'm telling you. Kind of scary."

She made a face.

He stepped back, palms up. "Just saying."

Now Troy was going too far. This made her mad. "Don't let a rumor like that get started, Troy. You know Christopher isn't weird—well, no more than any little brother would be. If he was trying on girls' perfume—which I don't believe he was—it would have been for a very good reason."

He shrugged. "Could be. Maybe he's buying it for his girlfriend."

Emily gasped. Surely, he wouldn't buy something so personal for Bailey already. "I doubt it."

"Look, just forget I said anything."

"Have you told anyone else?"

Silence.

"Troy?"

"No one else, just you."

"Swear?"

"Are we allowed to do that?" he asked.

She rolled her eyes. "Promise?"

"Promise."

"Hey, the swing is open," he said as Christopher and Bailey walked away. "Want me to push you?"

Emily reluctantly nodded and followed. She would get to the bottom of this. But she didn't like Troy making a big deal out of it. Besides, Troy had hardly acted like he missed her while he was gone, so she wasn't happy with him anyway. He was treading on thin ice.

Christopher had better not embarrass her in the youth group. Or he would pay. Big time.

CHARLOTTE WALKED BACK UP to the table to get some apple caramel pie, but it was gone. So she walked over to the cherry-berry. There were only two pieces gone from it. That was odd. Her cherry-berry pies were always the first to go.

"So, are you baking a lot of sugar-free pies these days for Bob?" Karen Ellis asked. Solid as a rock, Karen stood in front of her, eyes shining, empty plate ready for another go-around.

"I do bake some for him, yes."

"I've never tried that," Karen said. "So do you just make the pie the same as normal, but leave out the sugar?"

Charlotte had no idea why Karen wanted to talk about this just now. Then understanding hit her. She leaned over and placed her hand on her friend's arm.

"Oh, Karen, do you have diabetes?"

Her eyes grew wide. "Oh my, no. I just wondered because I tried a piece of your cherry-berry pie, and I could taste the difference. That's all."

Alarm shot through Charlotte. She hadn't made a sugar-free pie for the social.

"Oh, well, I, uh—" she stuttered.

Just then someone called out to Karen. "Sorry. Gotta go." She strode away with determined steps.

Charlotte looked around and then cautiously scooped a piece of cherry-berry pie onto her plate, turned and took a small bite.

After one small taste, she considered asking Bob if they could move out of state. She'd left out the sugar.

She eased the pie plate into her hands and headed for their car, trying to remember what might have gone wrong. It must have happened when she was all upset over Hannah instead of paying attention to her recipe.

Her pastor stopped her. "Charlotte, surely, you're not leaving so soon?"

"No, no, just had to run out to the car for a moment."

"Everything all right?"

"Why, yes. Why do you ask?"

"I've just noticed that you and Hannah haven't talked to one another today. Very unusual for the two of you." He gave her that peering-deep-into-your-soul look as only pastors can.

"Oh, uh, we're fine. Just keeping busy." She wasn't about to tell him. She had tried to make amends and Hannah obviously wasn't up for it. So that was that.

"Glad to hear it. You two are as solid as the church's foundation. Wouldn't want that shaken."

As solid as the church's foundation? Why didn't he just come out and tell her she was older than dirt?

His gaze shifted. "You're not taking your pie back to the car already, are you?" He was incredulous.

"Well, uh, the thought had crossed my mind." She squirmed trying to think how to word this so he wouldn't think her selfish—especially since last week's sermon had been on generosity of spirit.

"You're taking away my favorite pie?"

She squirmed some more.

Nancy Evans walked up and put a hand on him. "Now, Nathan, you leave her alone. Besides, your waistline doesn't need it." She winked at Charlotte. "She needs to save some for her family."

Charlotte smiled weakly and shrugged.

"How about I bake you your very own pie soon?" she asked, trying to declare a truce.

Pastor Evans brightened. "Okay, I'll release you with that pie, if you promise to give me another."

"Oh, you," his wife said, giving him a playful tap. "Thank you, Charlotte, you're very kind."

She gave a quick smile and headed toward the car like a cheetah on the run before anyone else could stop her.

Chapter
Twenty

The Stevenson family rushed to the breakfast table to get out the door in time for church.

"Christopher, we're waiting on you," Charlotte called up the stairs.

He came running down and plopped into his chair, everyone looking at him. Bob said a prayer and the family passed the biscuits and gravy, scrambled eggs and oatmeal.

Something seemed out of sorts. All this wonderful food but something didn't smell right. Charlotte got up from the table to investigate the countertop. Maybe she had left something out she shouldn't have. Finding nothing, she decided she must have imagined it.

One look at Emily, Sam and Bob said otherwise.

"What is that awful smell?" Emily asked, holding her hand up to her nose.

Sam looked over at Christopher and sniffed. "Is that you?"

Christopher, happily chomping away on a biscuit, hadn't noticed the fuss around the table. He looked at Sam in surprise. "Is what me?"

"That smell."

Christopher brightened. "You noticed?"

"Dude, the whole county could notice. You been rolling around in the barn or something?"

Christopher made a face. "Very funny. I bought some cologne at that garage sale I told you about," he said with absolute pride.

Jaws dropped. Utensils stopped clanging against dishes.

"You paid money for that smell?" Bob asked.

Snickers rippled around the table.

"What's wrong?" Christopher looked confused.

"Christopher, come with me," Charlotte said.

He got up from the table and followed her into the living room. "Something is definitely wrong with that cologne. Maybe it's too old or something. But at any rate, it is not a good scent for a seventh-grade young man."

"I don't want to smell like a seventh grader," he insisted.

"You don't?"

"No. I want to smell like a ninth grader."

Charlotte tried not to laugh. "Well, I can assure you, there are colognes available more suited to ninth graders. You go wash that off. One day you'll thank me."

"Oh, all right." Right now, he didn't look very thankful as he trudged himself up the stairs. Charlotte smiled and shook her head. This was a memory maker if she'd ever seen one.

"WHAT WAS THAT BOY THINKING?" Bob asked when he and Charlotte prepared for bed later that evening. Charlotte put her hand to her mouth to stifle her amusement. Bob walked over and let her press her laugh into his shoulder and they both had a good chuckle over it.

"For some reason he wants to be regarded as a ninth grader. He thinks girls like older boys." She shook her head. "Why do kids think they have to grow up so fast?" Charlotte grabbed a jar of cold cream and smeared the cream on her face.

"Weren't we the same way?" Bob asked.

Charlotte stopped spreading the cream and thought a moment. "I guess we were. Remember how you wanted to jack up that old Chevy of yours and your parents wouldn't let you?"

"Yeah, I remember," he said with a frown.

Charlotte blotted her face and walked over to him. Wrapping her arms around his waist she looked up at him. "I still thought you were the coolest guy around."

He looked down at her, pride from the glory days flashing in his eyes. "Oh, yeah?"

"Yeah."

"Now that I think about it, I probably shouldn't have told Christopher I didn't shave until I was eighteen."

Charlotte released her hold on her husband and walked back over to the dresser, trying to hide her smile.

"He'll get through this. One day he'll laugh about it." At least Charlotte hoped he would.

"Oh well. If he grows an inch or two this year, he'll feel better," Bob said. "But in case he doesn't—"

"Yeah?"

"—you'd better hide the makeup."

ONCE THE LIGHTS were out, Christopher stared at the ceiling. The family had had a good laugh at his expense. He sighed.

He snuggled into his pillow. Oh well—he had one more thing to try. He felt almost sure the taller shoes would do it.

Otherwise, he might have to live out the rest of his seventh-grade days without a girlfriend.

THE PROFESSOR dismissed the class. Sam grabbed his backpack and quickly exited. He had never been so glad to see the end of the class period. He was bored out of his mind and could barely keep his eyes open. Psychology. What did he care about analyzing people? What did he care about Pavlov's dog and learned responses? He didn't. It was as simple as that.

His mood darkened as he trudged across the campus lawn, and it had nothing to do with the smell of rain and gathering dark clouds. He didn't want to be here. College was a drag. He didn't have time to get to know that many people here, because everyone drove to campus and left. No great campus memories on his horizon.

Sam blew out a disappointed sigh and scuffed the ground with every step of his leather boots. Yes, he was glad he had met Katie, but she was just a friend at this point, and he still didn't want to live at home while going to college.

Why couldn't he get this settled in his mind? One minute he was thankful he wasn't going into major debt for school and the next minute—oh, he didn't know what he thought about anything anymore.

He popped into the library to check his e-mail. It never amounted to much, but occasionally he received something other than spam.

Dropping his bag on the floor beside him, he clicked into his e-mail account and waited for it to download. With a sweeping glance across the room, he saw students at tables surrounded by stacks of books, poring through pages, and others who sat in comfortable chairs and perused easier reads. Girls sat in clusters, with occasional giggles punctuating their whispers. Why did girls do that?

He looked at the computer screen again and saw an e-mail from Jordan Baker, his friend in San Diego. A quick read of the note said Jordan was struggling too. He wanted Sam to move back to California, even suggested they could get a place together, hang out, meet girls. Jordan had a great construction job and he was sure he could get Sam on because his uncle owned the business.

Sam leaned back in his chair and pondered the idea. He couldn't imagine what Jordan's parents thought about what their son was doing. Mr. Baker worked in finance for a major airline and Jordan's mom was a pediatric nurse. How did Jordan get out of going to college with parents like that?

Thoughts of San Diego crowded Sam's mind—the happy times with his mom, the blue skies, the surf—filling him with longing. Sometimes the idea of it seemed otherworldly. As though he had never really been there but only imagined it.

He glanced through the e-mail once more. He thought of his boring classes, the lame studying, the chores at the farm, his dull life.

Maybe going back to California wasn't such a bad idea after all.

PETE AND DANA had come out to the farm for dinner. While the grown-ups lingered at the kitchen table, Sam took Emily and Christopher into town for some ice cream.

"Guess the kids are tired of hanging around old people," Pete said.

"Can't blame them," Dana said.

"Hey, what are you implying?" Pete gave his wife an offended look.

She smiled. "Don't you remember being that age and wanting to hang out with your friends?"

He softened. "Yeah, I guess."

Charlotte set her coffee cup on the table and looked at them. "I suppose you haven't heard about our little episode with Christopher, have you?"

Pete shook his head. "What's up?"

Charlotte and Bob told them all about Christopher's fiasco with the bad cologne and how he was trying to look more manly for Bailey Winters.

"Uh-oh," Pete said.

Dana turned to him. "What?"

"I think I might have fueled that fire."

Charlotte frowned. "How do you mean?"

"He came to me for advice, and I told him girls liked

older men—or at least boys who appeared to be older." Pete shrugged. "I guess he thought of the rest."

"Oh, dear," Charlotte said, stifling a laugh.

Dana slugged his arm gently. "Peter Stevenson. You know how impressionable kids can be. What if he had worn that cologne in public? It could have dogged him all his high school years."

"How was I to know? I was just trying to help him out."

"You'd best leave the Dear Abby stuff to, well, Dear Abby," Dana said.

"You got any more pie, Mom?" Pete asked, holding up his dessert plate.

Charlotte suspected the sooner they changed the subject, the better. Maybe she ought to read that psychology book of Sam's she'd spotted around the house.

Chapter
Twenty-One

After volunteering at Bedford Gardens Wednesday afternoon, Charlotte headed back to the farm. On her way, she spotted Hannah outside, hanging laundry on her clothesline. Since Charlotte had no idea whether Hannah still wanted her to go to the getaway or not, she decided to get the matter between them settled once and for all.

She pulled the car into the drive and saw Hannah look up in surprise.

"Hi, Hannah."

"Hello." Hannah finished hanging the few clothes left, saying nothing more.

"I thought maybe I could have that mug of coffee now. Though I didn't bring my mug."

Hannah clipped the final pair of jeans on the line and then looked at her. "You're in luck. I just made a fresh pot for Frank."

"Is he in the house?"

"No, no. He went back out in the field. But I never know when he'll pop in for a quick cup of decaf."

Charlotte walked up to the house, hopeful she could get her friend back.

They settled at the table with cups in hand.

"Listen, Hannah. I'm not sure exactly what's happened between us, but I want to fix it."

Hannah gave her a cold look, but Charlotte trudged on. "I think it's my fault. I let Allison Cunningham put thoughts in my head that I shouldn't have."

Now she had Hannah's attention. "What kind of thoughts?"

"She mentioned something about me being too old to enjoy a girls' getaway and insinuated that you might take someone else."

"What? She told me if you were dragging your heels on this, you probably didn't want to go because you thought it was a silly thing to do at our age."

They stared at each for a long minute, and then both ladies started laughing.

"When did we start taking to heart things that Allison says?" Charlotte wanted to know.

"I have no idea. I think I was just so worried that you didn't want to go, and I couldn't think of anyone I would rather share this trip with. I was a little jealous too, because you always give to so many, and I wanted you to myself for a while. Oh, it just all got out of hand."

"I truly hesitated only because I was tired and didn't know how I could handle it all. I admit I was feeling a little pressured by you, but I see now that it's just because you really wanted me to go. At least the vitamins the doctor has me on seem to be helping. I'm feeling more energetic than I did before."

"That's great, Charlotte. I was so afraid I'd have to go on this weekend by myself—or make Frank go. He was praying we'd get things settled."

They discussed the matter a little further and decided to put the whole thing behind them.

Charlotte reached for her friend's hand. "I don't ever want to lose your friendship. We've been through too much together over the years."

"That we have."

"I'm sorry," they said simultaneously.

More laughs and hugs.

By the time Charlotte finished her visit, they were full swing into action for their upcoming trip. Two more days and they'd be on their way.

She waved goodbye to Hannah, feeling tons lighter, and then pulled into her own driveway. She tumbled out of her car and started for the back door when she remembered she had forgotten to get the mail. Needing the exercise, she trudged out to the mailbox.

The sun's warmth spilled over her, causing labored breathing and slowing of steps. Some days she felt her age more than she cared to admit. Still, the vitamins were helping.

Pulling open the mailbox, she reached in and lifted out the contents: a couple of bills, store advertisements, and a credit card envelope for Sam. She shook her head as she walked back to the house. These companies tried to tempt kids at a young age. She had every intention of tossing it into the trash can but decided she had no right to censor his mail. Trash or not, it was his mail to do with as he pleased. She merely had to trust him to make the right choices.

After all, Sam had a good head on his shoulders. He

wouldn't get sucked into the credit-card mania. She remembered that Emily had offered him some money recently. Charlotte still hadn't gotten to the bottom of that. Maybe it had something to do with his car repair.

It warmed her that Emily had been so thoughtful. These kids were truly growing up. And turning out to be responsible citizens at that.

Denise would be proud.

SOMETIMES LIFE didn't seem fair. Sam was working his butt off just to get some money together to cover his car repairs.

"Hey, Sam, would you run down to the coffee shop and grab me a cappuccino? Normal coffee won't cut it for the work I have ahead of me this afternoon," Uncle Bill said.

"Sure, Bill." His uncle had told him to call him Bill at work instead of Uncle Bill, so they would both feel more comfortable.

"Get yourself something while you're at it." Uncle Bill pressed money in his hand and Sam headed out the door.

A glance at his wristwatch told him everyone would be leaving in ten minutes. They had a lot of filing stacking up, so Bill had told him he could put in some extra hours to get it done. It looked as though they'd both be working late tonight.

Seemed Uncle Bill worked a lot of overtime. Sam wondered how Aunt Anna felt about that. The more he thought about it, the more he guessed that a college education might get the better jobs for the bigger stuff, but it also seemed to bring more headaches. Then again, maybe he was just looking for a way out of the rat race.

Sam stepped into the coffee shop, where smells of rich coffee and chocolate permeated the air. Since he was there he decided he'd get a mocha latte. He didn't think he'd have time to eat dinner for a while, so the mocha would tide him over until then. He was thankful his uncle was paying for it. Otherwise, he'd have to use his credit card. Since the car repair, he hadn't used his card much, other than occasional lattes on campus for him and for Katie.

After placing the order, he picked up his uncle's cappuccino and his own latte and then headed back to the office. Downtown was brimming with traffic, everyone trying to get out of the business district and go home where food and family waited for them.

He thought maybe that's what he wanted some day. A home with a family. Funny he should think that since he still had plenty of living to do before he got there.

He hoped if he had kids they would never know the pain of a divorce. When his dad walked out, it had hurt Sam. He thought his dad didn't like them. Sure, his mom had tried to explain that his dad hadn't stopped loving them, only her. That hadn't made sense to him either.

How could they be a happy family one minute and a broken one the next?

His mom had told them matters of the heart couldn't always be explained, but that didn't really make the pain go away. With hard work, he assumed love of the long-lasting type was possible. If his grandparents could make it work, he figured he could too.

"Here you go," Sam said, stepping into Uncle Bill's office. "And here's your change." He dumped the money in a pile on Uncle Bill's desk.

Bill looked up from his paperwork. "Oh, thanks."

Sam started to walk out of the office when Uncle Bill called to him.

"You're working late tonight, right?"

Sam turned around. "I was planning on it. Is that all right?"

"Sure. But why don't you sit down and join me for a quick break before we get back at it?" Uncle Bill pointed to an empty chair.

"Okay."

Sam walked over and eased into the leather chair across from Uncle Bill's large wooden desk. The desk was covered with files and paperwork.

"That doesn't look fun," Sam said.

Uncle Bill shrugged and took a sip of coffee. "It comes with the job."

Sam smiled and nodded.

"So how's school going so far?"

"Okay, I guess."

Uncle Bill studied him, making Sam uncomfortable.

"You hate it, don't you?"

Sam looked up with a start. "Why do you say that?"

"It's written all over you."

Sam slumped. "I just don't know what I want to do with my life."

"I understand that. I remember going through that myself."

"Really?" Sam couldn't imagine his uncle struggling with anything. "How did you figure it all out?"

"It took time, sorting through things in my mind. I focused on school, putting the time and study into it, but I didn't like it much—until Anna came along anyway. She definitely made things more interesting." He grinned and took another swig of coffee.

Sam grinned back.

"Is it college you don't like or that particular one?"

"I don't know, really. I'm just not sure if college is for me. But believe me, Grandpa has already given me many reasons for why college is for me."

Uncle Bill laughed. "Probably the same reasons he gave me back in the day."

"It's hard to stay at home and go to school, you know?" Sam said.

"Yeah. That's rough. Doesn't leave much room for partying." Uncle Bill winked. "On the other hand, it saves lots of money and it might help you to actually get some studying done, making the most of your college days. Hard to believe, but studying is really the best part of college. You know, to pay for something and actually learn from it."

Sam smiled. He knew that was right, but what college kid wanted to hear that? Responsibilities would come soon enough. Couldn't he have a little more time for fun until then?

"What else would you do with your life if you didn't go to college right now?" Uncle Bill asked.

Sam took a drink from his mocha and shrugged. "I've

thought over several things. Working, moving out on my own, maybe even going back to San Diego."

Uncle Bill watched him and stroked his chin thoughtfully. "I see." He paused a moment and Sam could tell he was trying to think of what to say next. "It's a time of real reflection, that's for sure," he said finally.

"Do you think I'm crazy to consider all those things?" Sam asked, truly wanting to know his uncle's thoughts.

"No. I believe it's a time of searching for many people. Just make sure you think everything through and don't let your emotions carry you. College is not a matter to consider lightly. To go or not to go decides your future."

"So you're saying that all people need to go to college to guarantee a successful future?" Sam asked.

"First of all, there are no guaranteed successes in this day and age. But I do believe college can help make that happen a little more easily. In my dad's day, people could skip college and it didn't seem to matter as much. But in today's world, you need a college degree to step into a lot of entry-level positions. In other words, the degree can get your foot in the door."

Sam knew that was true, though he wished it weren't. "Yeah, I guess."

"Still, you're the one who has to make it happen. Without studying, college is just another way to lose money."

Sam thought about that a minute and finished more of his mocha. "Well, I guess I'd better get back to filing."

"Yeah, if I don't get this done for tomorrow's deposition, I won't be going home at all tonight."

Sam got up and walked toward the door. Then he turned around. "Uncle Bill—er, uh, Bill?"

He looked up.

"Thanks."

Uncle Bill smiled. "You're welcome. Anytime you want to talk, just let me know."

Sam nodded and walked out the door. He wanted to believe things were crystal clear now, but the truth was he was more confused than ever.

Chapter Twenty-Two

The following afternoon, the breeze lifted Christopher's hair, cooling him off a little while he rode his bicycle. "Boy, that feels good. I've been so hot."

Dylan wiped his hand on the back of his neck. "Me too. I'll be glad when it cools off."

"You want to pull over?" Christopher pointed toward a big shade tree along the side of the country road.

"Sure." Dylan followed him to the tree where they propped their bikes up on the kickstands and settled beneath the umbrella of shade from the massive oak.

Christopher leaned his head back against the bark. "I'm bored. It's too hot to do anything."

"Yeah."

Christopher thought hard. There had to be something they could do.

"So do you still like Bailey?" Dylan reached for a long blade of grass and toyed with it.

"I guess so."

"You don't sound real happy about it," Dylan said.

"Girls are a lot of work."

"Yeah. I'm surprised she still likes you after you broke her wrist."

"Hey, I just threw her the ball." Christopher didn't like it that Dylan said that. "Besides, I don't know if she likes me or not."

"Well, she doesn't hate you. At least she talks to you. Usually, a girl won't pay any attention to you at all if she doesn't like you."

"How would you know?"

"I watch movies on TV."

They laughed.

"Are you going to game night Saturday night?" Dylan asked.

"Sure." He loved being part of the youth group.

"I guess you'll be trying to hang out with Bailey?"

Dylan said it as a question, but Christopher heard a sneer in there somewhere.

Christopher shrugged.

"I'm glad I don't have a girlfriend," Dylan said.

"Why?"

He shrugged. "Like you said, girls are hard work. They always want your attention. And they're bossy. 'Do this, do that,'" he said in a girly voice.

Christopher hadn't thought of that. "Bailey's not like that." He didn't think she was. Though he hadn't been around her enough to really know for sure.

"Well, just wait till you become boyfriend and girlfriend. That's when they really change. My stepdad says once they get you hooked, life as you've known it is over."

"Bet your mom liked that."

"She wasn't around at the time." Dylan laughed. "I think he's scared of her."

"So you've never really liked any girls?" Christopher asked. It almost made him laugh because he was sounding all experienced and he'd never liked a girl before Bailey.

"Nah." Dylan carefully shredded the blade of grass. "I'd rather hang out with you or my dog."

"Thanks. I think."

They laughed the kind of laugh that good friends share on a summer's afternoon beneath the canopy of an old oak tree.

"Do you ever wish you could be older?" Christopher asked.

Dylan thought a minute. "Not really. I don't mind being a kid. When you're old, you have to work all the time, take care of whiny kids and all that."

Christopher hadn't thought of that. "Yeah, you're right. I'd hate that." He considered it a little longer and absently rubbed the practically hairless skin above his lip.

He finally said, "I'm glad we're kids too."

Another rub under his nose. Still, part of him couldn't wait to grow a mustache, or grow taller, or develop muscles, or . . .

"WHAT'S THE MATTER with you?" Sam asked later that night when Christopher walked down the hallway toward his room.

"The youth group is having a game night Saturday at

Bailey's house, and school starts next week. I need new shoes. My old ones practically have a hole on the bottom."

Sam put his arm around his little brother's shoulder. "I see. Do you have any money for new ones?"

"Yeah, but Grandma never has time to take me to the mall."

"Tell you what. I only have morning classes tomorrow and no work, so how about I take you in the afternoon, after lunch?"

Christopher brightened. "You mean it?"

Sam gave his brother a swift pat on the back. "Sure I mean it, doofus. I'll swing by and pick you up around one o'clock."

"Thanks, Sam. You're an awesome brother."

Sam grinned. "I do my best." He walked away feeling pretty good. He hadn't spent much time with Christopher lately, so it would be good to have some one-on-one brother time. Catch up on things. He'd make sure Christopher had given up the makeup idea for good. In the meantime, Sam could get his mind off his own problems.

AFTER LIGHTING a pumpkin-scented candle, Charlotte plopped into her chair and pulled out her embroidery.

"A little early for that, wouldn't you say?" Bob asked.

"Fall is just around the corner, you know. Besides, I miss having our windows open, so this makes me think of the country."

Bob grinned. "Yeah, can't do without the air-conditioning in this heat."

"Exactly."

Someone knocked at the front door.

"Wonder who that is," Bob said, starting to rise.

"I'll get it, honey. You just watch your movie." Charlotte put aside her embroidery and headed for the door.

Hannah practically spilled through the door when Charlotte opened it.

"Can you stand it? We're leaving tomorrow!" Her eyes were bright and sparkly. Charlotte couldn't remember when she'd seen her this excited.

Charlotte chuckled. "I suppose you're all packed and ready to go?"

Hannah's eyes widened. "Of course. Aren't you?"

"Most of it is done. I'm waiting for the last load of laundry to dry. Then I'll pack the blouse I'm waiting on, and I'll be finished."

Hannah nodded. "I thought it might be best if we took off around ten o'clock. Give us time to have breakfast, say goodbye, and get the car loaded, without too much stress and rush. Then we'll have a beautiful day for driving there. Not to mention the entire afternoon and evening to walk around Appleton." She obviously needed this mini-vacation as much as Charlotte.

"Sounds heavenly," Charlotte said.

"I'm so glad you're coming, Char."

"Yeah, me too. We're gonna have such fun."

"Well, I'd better get going. I was just too excited to stay put and had to come over." She leaned in and gave Charlotte a hug. "See you tomorrow."

She rushed out the door and down the walk with a wave.

Charlotte smiled after her and thanked God for blessing her with such a wonderful friend.

"Sure am glad you two patched things up," Bob said when Charlotte rejoined him.

"Yeah, me too." She couldn't imagine her life without Hannah in it.

WHILE FINISHING UP her packing, Charlotte prayed for her family. She knew they would be fine without her, but the question was would she be fine without them?

Everyone had been so busy these days—she missed their evenings together. She thought of Sam going to college, Emily's mind already on college, and Christopher's eyes opening to girls.

She smoothed over a pair of pants and sighed. It all went so fast. Opening her drawer, she rummaged through the folded clothes and came upon her bathing suit. She couldn't believe she still had it. When was the last time Charlotte had tried to go swimming? It wasn't her favorite thing to do, but Hannah had insisted. It seemed the bed-and-breakfast had a lovely pool out back surrounded by a beautiful flower garden. They had to swim, if only one time, Hannah had said.

Charlotte had tried the bathing suit on last week, so she knew it still fit. She folded it carefully and laid it in her suitcase with her other things.

She was really going on this trip. With a prayer heavenward, she asked the Lord to help her enjoy it—not only for herself but also for her friend's sake.

THE NEXT MORNING, Christopher stepped through the back door into the kitchen. Lightning curled around his feet. He bent down and stroked his brown tabby, and then filled her food and water bowls.

Charlotte watched with appreciation how her young grandson was growing.

Placing the bowls on the floor, he swung around and faced Charlotte, who was holding her luggage in her hand.

"Grandma, where are you going?"

She chuckled. "I'm leaving for my weekend trip with Hannah this morning."

He frowned and his shoulders slumped. "Already?"

"Don't you worry about him, Mom. He's worried about the food chain thing," Pete said with a laugh as he stepped into the room.

Charlotte wasn't so sure. "You knew I was going, Christopher."

"Yeah, I just didn't know it was so soon." He looked as though he'd lost his best friend in all the world—or his last meal, she wasn't sure which.

Her heart clenched.

"Who's cooking while you're gone?" Christopher's voice was an octave higher than usual. "I'll lose five pounds in one weekend if Grandpa tries to cook again."

Charlotte relaxed a little. So Pete was right. Christopher was worried about his stomach. She walked over and gave him a hug.

"I'm sure you'll be just fine. I'll fatten you up when I get back."

He lifted a reluctant smile.

She studied him a moment. "What's different about you today?"

He clearly brightened. "Would you say I'm looking older?"

"You know, I think I would." She took an extra look at his upper lip. All was clear.

Pete nudged him. "See, I told you that you might sprout a muscle or two if you helped me with the hay."

Christopher smiled and stood taller.

Charlotte and Pete exchanged a glance.

Evidently, talk of looking older made him forget all about his stomach. She'd have to remember that when she got back.

The family gathered around her in the kitchen. Sam had already left for school but said goodbye before he left. Pete, Bob, Emily, and Christopher formed a circle with Charlotte and Bob said a prayer for her before she left. She heard Christopher's stomach growl and she wondered if she should have made extra cookies.

Just as Bob said "Amen," Hannah showed up at the back door, looking every inch a young girl eager to go out and play.

"Yoo-hoo, anybody home?"

Everyone laughed.

"Now you two behave yourselves," Bob said, giving his wife a playful hug and another quick kiss.

"No promises," Hannah said.

"Now I'm trusting you, Hannah, to take good care of my girl," Bob said, making Charlotte feel all warm inside.

"I will. She'll come back more rested than ever," Hannah called over her shoulder as she lifted Charlotte's suitcase into the trunk, and then slammed the lid closed with a thud.

"Bye, Grandma, have a good time," Emily said, waving.

"Thank you for your help, Emily. I'll pick you up something while I'm gone."

"You don't need to do that, Grandma. I'm glad to help."

Christopher waved, but his expression said he wasn't happy about this.

Pete gave a hearty wave, and then headed back to the barn. Toby barked and circled near the car, no doubt wondering where Charlotte was going without the family.

Once more, Hannah and Charlotte waved. Then Hannah edged her car out of the drive and onto the road. "See, that wasn't so bad, was it?"

Charlotte smiled, and then looked back once more, catching a glimpse of Christopher's face. She hoped he didn't lose five pounds while she was gone.

Chapter
Twenty-Three

"You all right?" Sam asked Christopher when they entered the Harding mall Friday afternoon.

"Yeah."

"You don't act like it." Sam made a mental note to stop by the pretzel place on their way out. He could smell the salt and baking bread as they walked by, the temptation hammering his senses.

Christopher shrugged and continued to shuffle along.

"Is it because Grandma left?"

"No," he said a little too quickly. Probably didn't want Sam to think he was a baby or something.

"Hey, I'm going to miss her too."

Christopher turned to him and brightened a little, a tinge of skepticism in his eyes. "You are?"

"Sure I am. No one else in our house can cook—except for Emily and she doesn't cook meat."

"Exactly." Christopher looked as though someone finally understood his pain.

Sam smiled. "At least it's not for long. She'll be back on Sunday. Then we'll be back to eating good grub."

"Yeah." His spirits seemed to perk up at that.

"In the meantime, we can eat junk food." Sam winked.

Christopher's feet lifted higher now when he walked, and a smile tugged on his mouth.

"Let's go in here. They have cool shoes," Sam said, pointing to the store. "Listen, while you're in here, I'm gonna run into the game store next door. I'll be back in a second. If I'm not done before you are, come next door."

"Okay."

Christopher was relieved. He wanted to pick out the shoes by himself. After a while, he settled on a pair of boots with square heels about two inches high. It made him feel older just trying them on.

He went up to the register. One guy rang up his purchase while a girl stuffed his shoebox into the bag. Sam walked into the store. And it was lucky for Christopher that Sam did because when Christopher reached for his wallet, it wasn't there.

"What's the matter?" Sam asked.

"I don't have my wallet." Christopher patted his pockets for a sign of his wallet but came up empty.

The line behind them grew and the cashier looked a tad impatient. "Guess I'll have to put them back," Christopher said.

"Don't do that. I'll take care of it for now and you can pay me back later," Sam said. He slipped his credit card from his wallet.

Christopher took the bag and thanked the cashier. As they walked out of the store, he thanked Sam.

"What do you think you did with your wallet?" Sam asked.

"I don't know for sure, but maybe it's at home. I thought I put it in my pocket, but last I remember, it was on my dresser."

"I hope that's it," Sam said, "and that you didn't lose it."

"Yeah, me too."

They passed on the pretzels on their way out the door. Sam said he wasn't hungry anymore.

Sam was quiet on the way home. Christopher wondered if he was mad that he had to bail him out. He'd pay Sam back right when they got home.

He sure hoped he could find his wallet.

BY THE TIME Christopher and Sam got home, Sam was feeling worse than ever. His credit-card debt kept growing and he didn't know how he was going to climb his way out. When he went to his bedroom, he plopped on the bed and tried to think things through. He was already working extra hours, and he couldn't afford any more, not with school.

He turned over and spotted something that had fallen from his nightstand onto the floor. A letter or something. He reached for it and picked it up.

His credit card statement.

Grandma must have put it there. He couldn't imagine why she hadn't given him a good talking to. Maybe she thought it was an advertisement. Lucky for him.

He ripped open the envelope and stared with disbelief at the balance. How had he gotten so out of control? Just a little here, a little there. He didn't think it would amount to much. And Christopher's purchase wasn't even listed there. He forced himself to breathe.

"I found it," Christopher said, standing at his door, waving his wallet. "Here you go, that should cover it." He laid some bills on Sam's bed. "Thanks again, Sam."

"You're welcome, dude."

Christopher walked back out. At least that purchase was taken care of. Sam picked up the money and stuffed it into his wallet. Having cash in his pocket made him feel lots better. He grabbed the phone and punched in some numbers.

"Katie, want to meet for coffee, say, at about six at the campus coffee shop?"

"Sure."

"I'll see you then."

He hung up the phone, feeling better. Yes, he would have to buy some coffee, but now he had a little cash.

ALL THE WAY TO APPLETON, Charlotte and Hannah were giddy with excitement. They chattered incessantly about the shops they planned to visit and the fun they were sure to have over the weekend.

They turned onto the winding lane that led up to the expansive bed-and-breakfast. Along the way, they took in a sweeping view of the manicured lawn, the generous mounds of mulch in raised flowerbeds, and the colorful flowers bursting from large pottery tubs on the porch.

"Oh, my." It was all Charlotte could manage.

"Didn't I tell you this would be restful?" Hannah shoved

the car into park and cut the engine. They hopped out, gathered their luggage, and hauled it up the porch steps to the red brick house. Subtle vines crept and curled along brick crevices, around windows and door frames, giving the place a cozy ambiance.

Charlotte could already feel her body transform. Her shoulders relaxed, her thoughts untangled, her steps slowed. Hannah was right; she did need this weekend.

The foyer housed a thick-cushioned sofa and love seat with plump decorative pillows, a couple of inviting rocking chairs, hardwood flooring with plush area rugs, bushy green plants in stylish pots, soft overhead lighting and cozy lamps on lamp stands. Assorted magazines lined the coffee table. Fresh coffee stirred the senses and ample coasters invited coffee breaks and visits.

Charlotte and Hannah looked around and tried not to gape.

"Good afternoon. May I help you?" The middle-aged woman behind the counter looked friendly and relaxed.

Hannah explained her win and before the two could release their breath, they were in their room, gawking at the amenities and, as good friends often do together, laughing over their good fortune.

"This will be a weekend we'll never forget, Charlotte. I can feel it," Hannah said, putting away her luggage and tidying up the area by her bed.

"I'm sure it will be. I'm so glad we got our misunderstanding settled."

"Me too. You've been a wonderful friend through the years, Charlotte." Hannah walked over to her and put an arm around Charlotte's shoulder. "Now, let's go get started. Time's a wasting."

The two friends walked out of the room together and Charlotte felt ten years roll off her shoulders with every step.

A hint of fall tinged the air. The sky blazed blue and sunlight scrubbed the town clean. Hannah and Charlotte spent the afternoon walking in and out of dress shops and craft corners.

When their feet had taken all they could stand, they went to a restaurant that served homemade meals, complete with coffee and pie. Charlotte couldn't imagine eating such good food without having to prepare it herself and clean up afterward.

"To think I almost missed out on this. It has been a marvelous day from start to finish."

Hannah finished a bite of her peach pie. "Hasn't it, though? I knew you would enjoy it. We both needed this." She looked around, then back at Charlotte. "I love Frank— you know that—but sometimes the stress of juggling everything—husband, church, home, all that—wears on a body."

"Yes, I agree."

"Sure you do. You have all that I have plus the additional burden of caring for grandchildren. I can't imagine it."

"I wouldn't call them a burden, really. They truly are a blessing."

"Oh, I know that. I just mean it can't be easy. You had your life all settled and into the rhythm of empty nest when you got the call about Denise. I know you're thrilled to have the kids there, but I also know it's a challenge on some days."

"That's true. You'd think by the second time around, we'd have it all figured out."

Hannah shook her head. "I don't see how. Every kid is different. What works for one doesn't necessarily work for the other—or so they tell me."

Charlotte smiled at her. "You know, Hannah, you have been almost as much a part of our kids' and grandkids' lives as we have."

Hannah lifted a grateful smile. "Thank you for that, Charlotte. You know I love your family as though it were my own."

"And vice versa." Charlotte finished the last of her blueberry pie. "That was absolutely heavenly. And the coffee. My goodness, it's good."

Hannah nodded with appreciation. "And to think we're just getting started."

Two more days of peace, quiet, and rest. Charlotte could only imagine it. She gave barely any thought at all to her family and whether they would be all right.

Barely any thought at all.

WITH COFFEE IN HAND, Sam and Katie slid into their seats at the coffee shop. The aroma of coffee blends and chocolate added warmth to the setting, making Sam feel better already. Anything to forget his debt for now.

"So what's up with you?" Katie asked after a sip from her cup.

"Just needed to get out of the house, you know?"

"Yeah, I know." There was a moment of silence. Katie went on, "I've been working on eBay stuff all day."

"Oh man, I never visit that site. I'd be buying stuff all the time."

She smiled. "I don't buy nearly as much as I sell."

That caught his interest. "Oh? What kind of stuff do you sell?"

"Are you kidding? They take everything. It amazes me what people want to buy there. And they seem to pay more there than they do at the store. For instance, my dad is a pharmaceutical sales rep and he gets these pens and gives them to me. I sold some of them on eBay and paid for my textbooks from the earnings on those pens! Can you believe it?"

Okay, now she really had his interest. "Wow, I had no idea."

"I'm telling you, if you need some extra cash, it's the place to go."

"I could use some extra cash. Don't know if I have anything worth selling, though."

"How about old toys, collection stuff. Anything you want to get rid of."

"I do have some baseball cards that I've been collecting since I was a kid. Gave up on it, though. I heard several of them are worth some money."

"Well, there you go," she said, taking another drink from her cup. "Just make sure you get them appraised first, so you ask enough for them."

"Wow, this is a great help, Katie. Thank you. I knew there was a reason I wanted to hang out with you tonight." He laughed.

"You needed a reason?" She fluttered her lashes.

He raised an eyebrow. "I guess not."

There may be more to this girl than meets the eye.

"How you doing in Psych class?" she asked.

"Okay, I guess. Don't really see how Pavlov's dog has anything to do with me." He took a drink from his latte.

"I think the conditioned response thing is pretty interesting."

"Yeah, I've experienced that lately. I see my credit-card bill and break out in a cold sweat. That's a learned response, isn't it?"

Now she laughed. "You're a pretty smart guy, Sam Slater."

"You think?"

"Yes, I do."

The sincerity on her face made him feel smarter. Maybe this college thing wasn't so bad after all.

✎ Chapter
Twenty-Four

T he next day just before lunch, Sam rummaged
through his closet in search of things he could sell
on eBay. So far he had an old baseball and a
catcher's mitt, a handful of baseball cards that he needed to
have appraised, a Battleship game, a KerPlunk game, and
Power Rangers and Batman action figures.

Tenderly, he picked up the KerPlunk game. The marbles
rattled around in the plastic container. His mother's smile
flashed through his mind. He had beaten her again. She
humored him with her usual, "Oh, I just can't win that
game with you," but deep down, he knew she let him win
most of the time. Boy, he missed those days. He set the
game aside from the others. He wasn't ready to part with
that one just yet.

More rummaging produced a couple of belts he no
longer wore, some CDs he no longer listened to since he
had his phone, and a few pairs of jeans he had outgrown.
Once his pile was in order, he would set up an eBay
account as a seller and go to work creating listings of items
he wanted to sell. He'd have to take pictures and post
them.

"Sam, come and eat."

His sister's voice wafted up the stairway and barely reached his room. Why hadn't he gone out for a hamburger while he had the chance? Now he'd be stuck eating some kind of veggie burger or who knew what.

He sighed. If he weren't so hungry, he'd skip the meal entirely, but his stomach told him there was no use in resisting.

Once downstairs, he saw that everyone else was in place around the table. Christopher's chin was slumped into the palm of his hand. Grandpa's face was pulled into a frown. This did not look like a happy place.

They needed Grandma.

Emily walked over to the table and placed a deep kettle of some kind of soup in the middle.

Didn't smell bad. Sam noticed that even Christopher lifted his eyes toward the pot with hope.

Emily placed the pot holders at the side of the kettle, slipped into her chair, and looking quite pleased, said to Grandpa, "Would you say the prayer for us, please?"

There was a certain five-star polish about it all. Sam felt they should be flipping open linen napkins before diving into the soup.

After prayer, Emily filled everyone's bowls. He hoped she wouldn't be offended if they didn't finish what she gave them.

"Looks like a, um, fine meal you've got here, Emily," Grandpa said.

When she scooped the soup into the ladle, the aroma passed among them, and Sam had to admit it smelled pretty good. The look on Christopher's face said he'd give it a try.

"What's this soup called?" Grandpa asked. Sam could hear caution in his voice. Seemed as though all of them were a tad concerned. Uncle Pete was lucky he had married and had gotten out of their kitchen in the nick of time.

"It's chili—without the meat," Emily said with a smile.

Sam stared into his bowl. It was thick with assorted beans, corn, and spices, and he recognized a few chili peppers.

That didn't sound too bad. Sam picked up his spoon at the same time as Christopher. And as though they were standing before a firing squad, they shared a "last" glance. One spoonful down the hatch.

They'd survived it. The brothers paused. Christopher was still kicking and as far as Sam could tell, his heart was still beating too.

Not only had they survived it, but the chili also tasted downright good.

Another bite. And another.

"Sis, this is pretty good," Sam said with pure admiration.

"Well, what did you expect, dog food?"

Here he was trying to compliment her and she looked put out. Sisters. He'd never understand them.

Christopher was eating fast enough for all of them.

"Slow down there, cowboy," Grandpa said, the twitch of a grin on the corners of his mouth. "From what I can see, there's plenty more in that pot."

"Yes, Grandpa." Christopher kept a slower but steady pace.

Emily sat back in her seat, glanced around the table and looked very pleased with the family response.

Maybe they'd survive Grandma's absence after all.

CHARLOTTE AND HANNAH slipped through the door into Sylvia's Smile in Style, a dress boutique.

An apple scent greeted them from a shelf of lotions at the entrance. Racks of elegant dresses stood before them through the center of the store and the side walls held sweater displays and shoes.

"Good afternoon, ladies." A woman of around thirty lifted a warm smile. "May I help you with anything?" Dressed in a stylish black dress and houndstooth jacket, she looked the perfect model for the store.

"We're just looking," Hannah said.

"If you need anything at all, please let me know. I'll be happy to assist you," the woman said. And with that, she slipped away, leaving Charlotte and Hannah to enjoy the store without further interruption.

"Oh, my goodness, look at these shoes, Charlotte." Hannah held up a cute pair of jeweled shoes, sparkles everywhere.

"You going to wear those to the church hayride?" Charlotte giggled.

"I was thinking more of a night on the town with Frank," she said with a twinkle in her eyes.

"Good luck with that one. He's just like Bob and they're not big on nights on the town."

Hannah sighed. "Yeah, you're right."

Charlotte felt bad for saying that. She'd sucked the joy right out of Hannah's face.

"But you know, maybe Frank would want to go out on the town if he saw you all dolled up in a cute dress and sparkly shoes like that." Charlotte wiggled her eyebrows.

Hannah brightened. "You think? I've saved some money, so I could get something if I want to."

"I think you should look around and see if there's anything you want. This is our weekend." Feeling younger than she had in years, Charlotte looped her arm through Hannah's as they moved deeper into the store.

"Oh, I think you should try this on, Charlotte. It would go nice with your hair." Hannah held up a cute little blue number. There was a scoop in the neck, a wide belt to cinch the waist and a flirty skirt.

"My heavens, Bob would keel right over if I showed up in that one."

"Wouldn't hurt to shake these guys up a little," Hannah said, placing the dress back on the rack.

They laughed and looked through more clothes until their stomachs told them it was time to eat.

"We're going to hit the makeup store next," Hannah said with a glint in her eye.

"Hannah Carter, what has gotten into you?" Charlotte wanted to know.

"Life." Now she looped her arm through Charlotte's. "This weekend, we're going to live again."

"COME ON IN, EMILY," Uncle Bill said when he opened the door.

Pigtails flying, Madison and Jennifer ran over to her and squeezed her legs.

"I wish we could stay here with you," Madison said with a pout.

Emily smiled and scrunched down to hug the girls. "We'll get to play next time."

"But we have to go to school next week," Madison said.

Jennifer's eyes betrayed her. The mere mention of school made her eyes sparkle.

"School will be fun, won't it, Jennifer?" Emily asked.

Jennifer nodded her head vigorously, causing Emily to laugh.

"All right, you two. Give Emily room to breathe." On a Saturday afternoon, Aunt Anna was dressed to the nines in a pair of black pants and a tasteful slipover with matching shoes and jewelry.

"Okay, Emily, you have my cell-phone number." Aunt Anna adjusted the black Gucci bag on her arm.

Emily nodded.

"We'll be shopping for a little while, but we'll be back before dinner." She turned to Madison. "Did you girls put away the grapes you had out earlier?"

Madison nodded.

"Good." Aunt Anna looked back at Emily. "It seems the kitchen is all clean, so you really need only to look after Will."

They quickly said their good-byes and Emily relaxed once they were gone. Something about Aunt Anna just made her nervous. She walked over to Will who was sitting up and playing with blocks on the floor. Bending down, she sat with him and shifted the blocks around, stacking and maneuvering with him while he babbled and squealed.

Finally, she got up and walked over to the computer. She could still see Will from where she sat, so she started an email to Troy. They hadn't talked a lot since he got back from his trip, and she decided to see if he was online.

He was.

"Hey, what's up?" She loved messaging him.

"Not much. Thinking about going to the mall later. Want to go? Then we could go to teen game night or go to dinner, maybe even catch that movie we never got to see."

Her spirit plunged. She would love to go but she'd be babysitting for a while and then she needed to help at home with Grandma gone.

"I wish I could, but I'm babysitting." She glanced over at Will who had crawled slightly away from the area but was still in view.

"Oh," he said. "Too bad."

"Why haven't you called lately?" She didn't want to sound like a nagging girlfriend, but she was curious.

"Been busy."

That was his only response. That smelled like trouble to her. Was he going to dump her? Had he met someone else on his trip?

"Busy doing what?" she tried to act nonchalant, but that was hard to do over the computer.

"Working at the steakhouse."

"Oh." He was dumping her; she could feel it. Her stomach roiled and she thought she might get sick. Not that they were all that serious, but she did like Troy, and the thought of rejection hurt to the core. She didn't know what to say from here. Evidently he didn't either because he hadn't responded to her.

"Well—" he began.

She heard a strange gasping noise that startled her. She became frantic when she scanned the room and didn't see Will. She ran to the kitchen entrance a few feet away and found him on the floor, gasping for breath.

White-hot adrenaline shot clear through her. Her hands shook with the phone as she punched in the numbers 9-1-1 and scooped Will into her arms. She rattled off the address and problem, hung up, then turned the baby over. She remembered from class to apply the Heimlich maneuver as long as the child was still conscious. If there was no response, then apply CPR. While supporting his neck and head, Emily gave Will five back slaps on his upper back with her hand. Tears streamed down her face and she tried to catch her breath, to stay calm and in control. She couldn't lose it now. Will needed her. "Please, please, please, Will." She swallowed hard, refusing the panic that screamed to take over. Emily turned him over and gave him one, two, three, four, five chest thrusts.

Fortunately, the EMTs had been nearby and they arrived just as a grape popped out of Will's mouth and his breathing was restored.

She sat on the floor, holding the baby tight as he wailed and she cried along with him.

The EMTs barged through the front door. "Ma'am?"

"Back here," she called with a shaky voice.

A man and woman entered the kitchen, jangling with medical gadgetry.

"Everyone all right?" the man asked.

Emily wiped her face and nodded. "This is the baby who was choking." She looked around the floor. "There it is."

She pointed to the grape on the floor. "He had choked on a grape." More tears slipped down her face.

"You should never feed a baby grapes," the woman said.

"I didn't. He must have found it on the floor."

The man and woman checked Will over, much to his distress.

"Looks to me like the little fella is gonna be okay," the man said. "You did everything right, young lady. If you're ever in this situation again, though, make sure you take care of the kid before you call 9-1-1 unless you're sure there is time. Then call the first chance you get."

Just then Uncle Bill and Aunt Anna walked through the door. Jennifer and Madison stood mute beside them, staring wide-eyed at little Will. Uncle Bill's face flushed red. Aunt Anna pushed past everyone and ran to Will. Her eyes looked wild with fear, her face pale. She grabbed hold of the crying baby and gently rocked him back and forth, holding him as though she'd never let go. "What happened?"

The EMT man looked at her. "And you are?"

"The parents. This is our niece, who was babysitting our son," Uncle Bill said. "What's the problem?"

"No problem now," the woman assured them.

"This little gal saved your son's life," the man interjected.

As the details were given, Aunt Anna's face turned from pale to ashen. Her body trembled. Uncle Bill tried to take the baby from her so she could calm herself, but she refused to let Will go. With the infant in hand, Aunt Anna settled on the sofa. The EMTs left and for a moment, no one said a word. Finally, the baby's cries had softened to an occasional gurgle and hiccup. Aunt Anna looked over at Emily.

"Are you all right?" she asked.

"I'm fine. Just a little shaken," Emily said.

"I don't know what to say. One of the girls must have dropped a grape on the floor—" Aunt Anna's words seemed to stick in her throat. "I should have checked—"

Uncle Bill put his arm around her shoulder. "Now, honey, there's no point in casting blame. What's done is done. We've all learned something from this. One thing I've learned is that we have the best babysitter in town." He grinned at Emily.

"What made you come back so soon?" Emily asked.

"I left my wallet at home," Uncle Bill said.

"Lucky for us," Aunt Anna said with a cross voice.

"Now, Anna—"

Aunt Anna cut him off. "How did he get that grape in the first place? Weren't you watching him?"

Shame sliced through Emily. Her head hung low. "I was on the computer."

"What?" Aunt Anna practically shrieked. "Well, no wonder he got hurt. We're paying you to watch our son, not play on the computer."

Another tear trekked down Emily's cheeks. "I'm sorry, Aunt Anna."

Uncle Bill put a hand on Aunt Anna's shoulder. "Now, Anna, you know it wasn't anyone's fault. It just happened."

"But it wouldn't have happened if—"

"Anna," Uncle Bill's voice was more stern now. "Let it go. The important thing is that Emily knew what to do in an emergency situation. And for that I'm grateful."

Aunt Anna seemed to soften. She clutched Will tight

against her chest and kissed his head, tears streaming down her own face.

"Is he gonna be okay, Mommy?" Madison wanted to know.

"Yes, honey, he'll be fine," Aunt Anna said.

With sickening clarity Emily realized Aunt Anna was right. If she hadn't been on the computer, she could have stopped Will from putting the grape into his mouth. She wouldn't blame them if they never let her near their son again.

Once everyone had calmed down, Emily said her good-byes, and as she got in the car she realized something else. If she hadn't taken that babysitting class, they could have lost Will forever.

Chapter
Twenty-Five

Christopher waved goodbye to Sam and turned to knock on the front door of Bailey's house.

The door creaked open and Bailey smiled brightly. "Hey, Christopher, come on in."

Stepping inside, he saw a lot of other kids from the youth group were already there.

"I thought you weren't going to come," Bailey said, walking him into the kitchen/family room where the others were mingling.

Her comment caused a flip in his stomach. Did that mean she would have been disappointed if he hadn't come? Just thinking that made him feel pretty special. Well, that and his new shoes.

"Are you kidding? I wouldn't have missed tonight."

Her gaze latched onto him and wouldn't let go. Suddenly, his neck and face felt hot. His stomach didn't feel so good.

"How's your arm?" he asked.

"It's fine. I hardly notice this thing anymore," she said, raising her cast. "I'll be out of it in no time."

She tried to put him at ease about the injury, and he liked that about her. Grandma said she was thoughtful, and he thought so too. He was sure lucky that she paid attention to him.

"You want something to eat?" she asked, pointing to the food on the kitchen island. "These are just appetizers till the burgers and hot dogs are finished grilling."

"Thanks." Christopher grabbed a paper plate and loaded on chips and dip, leaving the raw celery sticks, carrot slices, and broccoli to the more health-conscious teens in the group.

"Hey, Christopher." Dylan walked over to him, along with a couple of other guys.

Bailey walked away and joined a group of girls while Christopher chilled out with the guys. He was glad. He didn't want to hang around the girls all night.

"Hey, Chris, where's your sister?" Troy wanted to know.

"She didn't feel like coming tonight," Christopher said.

Troy didn't look happy about that, but Christopher figured he could take that up with Emily. He wasn't going to be their messenger boy.

He was going to tell Troy about how Emily had saved little Will today, but Pastor Vink called them to order for prayer for their meal.

After they ate, Pastor Vink led them through charades and a couple of other games before they all settled down to ice cream sundaes. Bailey cornered Christopher before he could join the guys.

"Let's sit here," she said, pointing to two chairs in the corner.

The bossy tone of her voice surprised—and scared—him. Made him think of his conversation with Dylan. Though he liked Bailey a lot, he wasn't ready to be bossed by any girl.

"Are you having fun?"

"Yeah," he said.

"Me too. I'm sure glad we moved here."

"Yeah," he said, spooning a bite of ice cream and chocolate into his mouth.

"You seem taller somehow," she said.

Pride zipped straight through him for having the insight to buy the boots with heels. "Must be a growth spurt," he said. He'd heard his grandma say that before about Sam and figured he'd be due to have one soon. But until then, the shoes would have to cover for him.

Bailey laughed. "Must be." A moment of quiet between them followed.

"I heard there was a back-to-school dance next Friday in the gym. Are you going?" she asked.

He scrunched his nose. "No way."

"Why not?"

He shrugged.

She noticeably slumped in her chair. He wondered why.

"Don't you like to dance?" she asked.

"Nah." He really liked this ice cream sundae, though. Bailey's mom sure knew how to make good food. Just like Grandma. He couldn't wait till she got back tomorrow.

"I think I'm going to go sit with the girls," she said, looking straight at him but moving nary a muscle.

He looked at her and nodded, wondering what that had

to do with him. Once he finished off his sundae he noticed she'd barely touched hers.

"What's wrong, don't you like it?" he asked, pointing to her bowl.

She stared at him, like something upset her.

"You okay?"

"I'm fine." She whipped around and stomped away from him.

He couldn't imagine what had gotten into her. Oh well. Mrs. Winters had said there was more ice cream, so he made a beeline for the kitchen.

EMILY HUGGED HER KNEES to her chest as she sat in the middle of her bed. The events of the day left her tingling with "what ifs." Unbidden tears streamed down her face once more. She couldn't shake the tension. Yes, Will was fine. She had done the right thing and gotten him through the whole ordeal. But what if she hadn't? What if she had refused to take that babysitting course? She wouldn't have had a clue as to how to save him when he was choking.

Not only that, but what if she could have spared him the whole ordeal by watching him and not typing on the computer? She wouldn't blame Aunt Anna and Uncle Bill if they never talked to her again.

The very thought of all of it made her ill. The course of history would have been changed had she not taken the babysitting course. His death would have greatly affected everyone in their family. His death would have changed her life for sure.

The clamoring thoughts bumped against one another, tangling with thoughts of her mother's death and how events shape people.

Curled in a ball, she rocked back and forth, trying to make sense of it all. Why do bad things happen? Yes, in this case, everything turned out all right, but still, it had happened. Could she have prevented it? She didn't want that kind of responsibility. It terrified her. She wasn't a hero. Aunt Anna was the hero for having had the foresight to make Emily take that babysitting class.

A knock sounded at her door. "Emily, can I come in?" her grandpa asked.

"Yes," she said.

The door slowly creaked open and he stood at the entrance, looking at her. "Are you all right?"

She nodded.

His steps lapped up the distance between them and he looked down at her. "I know your grandma is much better equipped to handle things like this, but if you need anything, just let me know, okay?"

"Thanks, Grandpa."

"I know you've been through a lot today. You saved a little boy's life."

She looked up at him through blurred vision. "I was on the computer when it happened, Grandpa. I should have prevented it." A flood of tears erupted onto her cheeks.

Grandpa eased onto the edge of the bed and reached for her. He pulled her into a gentle embrace.

After her tears were spent he looked at her. "Emily, we all make mistakes. Accidents happen. You could have been in the same room and glanced away and it still would have happened." He paused. "The best thing is that you learned from it."

She looked up. "Yeah, I'll never get on the computer again while I'm babysitting, that's for sure." She thought a moment. "And what if I hadn't taken the babysitting course?"

"You know, I heard it said once that a person's worst enemies are the words 'what if.' What if this happens or doesn't happen? You can worry yourself sick about it. The thing is you saved him. Period."

She tried to let the words sink in.

"Did you hear me?"

She nodded.

"Don't question it, Emily. God saw that you had the ability to help Will when he needed it. God sees the whole picture, remember. You were a part of that plan. He used you to save little Will's life, no doubt about it."

Those words made her feel better—as though she were part of something far bigger than herself. "Thanks, Grandpa."

"Now, if I were you, instead of sitting upstairs in my bedroom, I'd go out with Ashley and celebrate."

Ashley had been working all day, so Emily was sure her friend hadn't gone to the teen event tonight.

Emily wished she could go out with Troy, but he seemed so distant when they talked. In all the commotion, she couldn't exactly remember how they'd left off, so she'd thought he might call her, but he hadn't. She wondered if he'd gone to the teen activity tonight or if he'd gone to the movie. Christopher would tell her once he got home.

"Did you eat dinner?" she asked.

"Sam and Christopher are gone and you were gone, so I

just ate some leftovers. You're off the hook. Go call your friend."

She smiled and reached over to give her grandpa a hug. It was rare that he showed his soft side, so his sincerity made her love him all the more.

"Now I'd better go check on Toby. I saw her sniffing around in Sam's room, which probably means there are some dead French fries under his bed."

Emily scrunched her nose at the image.

He gave a grunt when he shoved himself off her bed.

Emily watched as her grandpa shuffled out of her room. She needed to wash her face, so she got up from the bed and followed her grandpa out of the room.

"Toby, you get out of there," Grandpa called out.

Emily chuckled, wet her face, patted it dry, and headed back toward her room. She glanced in at Grandpa in Sam's room and stopped in her tracks. He was reading something from Sam's nightstand and by the look on his face, he was none too happy. She hoped it wasn't Sam's credit card statement, but by the look of the writing on it from where she stood, things were going to heat up around the Stevenson household tonight.

Since she hadn't heard from Troy, it seemed a good time to call Ashley.

SAM HAD BARELY gotten through the front door when Grandpa called out to him. "Sam, come in the family room. I need to talk to you."

Sam stepped inside the room. No one was there but

Grandpa. The room smelled of buttered popcorn. That sounded good to Sam. He hadn't eaten in a while.

"Come over here and sit down," Grandpa said, motioning toward the sofa.

Guess the popcorn would have to wait. Sam walked over to the sofa and sat down. He couldn't imagine what was going on, but he could tell by the look on Grandpa's face that he was in trouble.

Grandpa reached for something on the stand next to him. "You want to tell me what this is about?" He was holding a long paper and Sam knew in a glance what it was.

Silence filled the distance between them until the cuckoo clock on the wall struck eight. Sam waited for the bird to stop coming out and the bonging to stop before he said anything.

"I got a credit card," he finally said.

"After all I've told you about them?" Grandpa shook his head.

"I'm sorry, Grandpa. I just needed some extra cash." He wanted to ask him what he was doing snooping around in his bedroom.

"For what, Sam?"

"For—for the car repairs." That was half-true. He hadn't gotten the credit card for the car repairs, but he did use it for them as well.

Grandpa rubbed his hand across the back of his neck. "Boy, what I'm trying to get you to see is that it will only breed more debt."

"I planned to pay it off each month." Boy, he wished he hadn't said that. Grandpa would pounce on that one for sure, and of course, his plans hadn't worked out that way.

"And have you?" Grandpa asked.

Sam stared at his fingers. "No, sir."

"That's what I'm talking about, Sam. They charge such horrendous interest that you can't ever catch up with your salary. If you needed help with your car, you should have told us. We could have helped you."

Sam looked up at him.

"I know, I know, I tell you I want you to pay for things yourself, learn responsibility. But that doesn't mean I won't help you when you have a real need. You could have paid us back without the interest."

Sam felt guilty thinking about the clothes and frivolous spending he'd been doing lately.

"It's up to you. You're a grown man now. Men your age are fighting for our country. So I'm going to leave this decision to you." Grandpa stared Sam straight in the eyes. "I'll help you if you decide you want some help figuring out a budget to pay it off as quickly as possible. Just let me know." With that, Grandpa picked up his TV remote and clicked it back on.

The discussion was over, but Grandpa had given Sam plenty to think about. Deep down he knew Grandpa was right.

Still, he just wasn't sure he was ready to give up the spending.

Chapter Twenty-Six

"Hey, Christopher, do you still like Bailey?" Dylan asked when he joined him in the Winters' kitchen, getting more ice cream.

"I guess so, why?"

Dylan's eyebrows rose two inches. "'Cause she sure is mad at you." He whispered it so Mrs. Winters wouldn't hear. She dipped the ice cream into their bowls and let them put on their own toppings.

"Mad at me? Why?" Christopher had no clue. Girls sure were hard to figure out.

Dylan shrugged. "I just heard her talking to the girls and she said, 'Oh, that Christopher makes me so mad.'"

"Maybe it was another Christopher," he said, taking a bite of ice cream and scanning the table for more toppings.

"Maybe," Dylan said skeptically. "But I don't know any other Christophers around here."

"Not much I can do about it if I don't even know how I made her mad."

Once Christopher and Dylan finished their ice cream, Pastor Vink led the group in devotions and game night came to an end. Christopher had enjoyed himself immensely.

The teens began filing out the front door one by one, each giving thanks and farewells to the Winters family for opening their home to them.

Christopher thanked them as well. He spotted Dylan's mom who was taking him home, and then he turned to Bailey.

"Bye, Bailey. See you at church tomorrow."

"Bye, Christopher."

Right then one of the teen girls walked past him and whispered, "Wow, that was a bit icy." Then she laughed.

He had no idea what she was talking about. Girls were so weird.

HANNAH AND CHARLOTTE stepped into a quaint restaurant in the town square. They had decided to splurge on their last dinner in Appleton. They were led to a corner table by a young man with a mustache as skinny as he was.

"Did you see his mustache?" Charlotte whispered with a chuckle, as they opened their menus.

"Yes."

"That made me think of Christopher and his rush to look grown up."

They both started laughing.

"Poor kid. It's a hard place to be," Hannah said, putting her linen napkin on her lap.

"It's easy to forget that. But he brought it all back," Charlotte said.

The waiter approached them and took their order.

Another laugh.

Hannah turned to Charlotte. "You know, when I was Christopher's age, I put on one of my mother's bras, stuffed it with toilet paper, and wore it to school."

Charlotte studied her. "No."

"Yes, I did. Then when we played dodgeball, the toilet paper slipped from the elastic and fell to the gym floor in front of the class. Fortunately, since everyone was busy playing the game, no one really knew where it came from."

Charlotte tried to stop laughing so she could catch her breath. "Stop."

"I never tried it again."

"Oh my. Only you, Hannah."

"I guess." She grinned as the waiter came with their food and they started eating. "I can't believe we are just now stopping to eat. If I ate this late every night, I'd weigh three hundred pounds."

"Me too," Charlotte said.

Through the course of their meal, they discussed Pete and Dana's wedding, Bill and Anna's kids and how Emily was doing babysitting, how Frank was feeling since the heart attack, and how Bob was handling Andy Weber at the store.

Once they had finished, they stepped outside beneath the glow of the moon and the street lamps as they walked the cobbled street back to their bed-and-breakfast, which was only a few blocks away.

"It's a perfect night," Charlotte said, gazing into the twilight sky.

"It is indeed."

Charlotte wondered what everyone was doing at home,

but she didn't bring it up. She didn't want Hannah to think she wasn't enjoying herself.

Back in their room, they settled on their beds and Hannah pulled out a brochure. "I thought we'd go to the spa tomorrow and also get a manicure and pedicure."

"Oh my. I've never had one of those," Charlotte said, glancing at her pathetic, weak, splintered nails. "Not much use for a manicure or pedicure on the farm."

"That's exactly why we need to do it," Hannah said, leaving no room for argument.

Getting comfortable on her bed, Charlotte stretched out her legs. "Feels good to rest my legs," she said. "This summer heat has kept me from walking for a while."

"Yeah, I've missed my walking partner," Hannah said.

"Oh, you. You haven't been walking either."

"I know. I like to blame that on you. Makes me feel better." Hannah grinned.

Charlotte propped her hands behind her head against the pillow and stared up at the ceiling.

"You still miss her, don't you?" Hannah asked gently.

"How did you know what I was thinking?" Hannah seemed to have a sixth sense about Charlotte and her thoughts of Denise.

"A certain look comes over you. I can always tell."

"I do miss her. I suppose I always will. She was my daughter. If only things could have been different. If we had been closer, I wonder . . ."

"You have to stop blaming yourself, Charlotte. It was what it was. You did the best you could as a parent and Denise made her choices. Now you have to let it go at that."

"I know you're right."

Silence filled the space between them.

"I've never told you this before, Charlotte. In fact, the only one who knows is Frank because I've never told anyone else."

Charlotte propped herself up on one elbow and looked at her friend. "What is it, Hannah?"

"We were married only two years at the time." Hannah's eyes took on a distant look. "I got pregnant."

Charlotte gasped. "But you said—"

Hannah cut off Charlotte's protest with an upheld palm. "Just hear me out."

Charlotte nodded and listened.

"I was pregnant. We didn't tell anyone because I was having some trouble, a little spotting, and I didn't want to jinx it." She looked at Charlotte. "The doctor told me I needed to rest. I tried. I really did. But you know me. I have trouble staying down for very long."

Charlotte nodded.

"So one day while resting in bed, I noticed how dusty the drapes in the bedroom were. I decided it wouldn't take much to launder them.

"So I got up, carefully took down the curtains and washed them. Once they were dry, I started to rehang them. Frank came home and caught me red-handed." She smiled. "He finished the hanging, but unfortunately, right after I got back in bed, I started cramping. It wouldn't stop."

"Oh, Hannah."

"Frank rushed me to the hospital and there we said goodbye to our only baby." Tears streamed down Hannah's cheeks now and, with tears of her own, Charlotte went to Hannah's side. She held her hand. Hannah looked up at her. "We never even knew if the baby was a boy or a girl."

"I'm so sorry," Charlotte said.

"The doctor said I probably would have lost the baby anyway, and mentioned some fancy medical term, but I wasn't convinced. I still blamed myself. And it also convinced me to do what my doctor said from then on. Which is why you also shouldn't feel guilty when your doctor tells you it's all right to rest now and then. Take time for you."

Charlotte nodded.

"Look, Charlotte, it took me a very long time to forgive myself. I kept thinking if only I hadn't done that, our baby would be with us today. I went through a terrible depression. I stopped eating. The counselor told me that without realizing it, I was not eating to punish myself for what I believed I had done to our baby. He helped me to see the futility in that thinking. It wouldn't bring the baby back. It was what it was. Nothing would ever change that."

Hannah turned to Charlotte. "That's the message I want you to hear, Charlotte. Stop blaming yourself. It won't change anything—but you."

Charlotte hadn't thought of that. Her guilt had changed her over time—making her doubt herself as a parent and grandparent on many occasions, making her depressed and lonely at times, even with so many family members around her.

"The weird thing is that I think I work through it and before I know it, the pain and guilt are back again," Charlotte said.

"I understand that. I went through that many times. It took a counselor to help me through."

Silence.

"I should have told you this long ago," Hannah said. "But it's a part of my past that was buried with our baby. Bringing it out is still painful."

By now both women were crying and hugging. Though Charlotte and Hannah had been the best of friends for quite some time, in that moment, Charlotte sensed they had connected on a deeper level—one mother's heart to another's.

"Thank you for sharing your heart with me, Hannah. That had to be a hard thing to do, and I cherish your courage."

"Just put it to good use and let go of the guilt about Denise. Then I'll be glad I shared it."

"I'll work on it," Charlotte said with a smile before she gave Hannah one final hug. And indeed she would.

"Now," Hannah said, "Let's go for a swim."

Chapter Twenty-Seven

F or I know the plans I have for you," declares the Lord, "plans to prosper you and not to harm you, plans to give you hope and a future." Pastor Evans barely had Jeremiah 29:11 out of his mouth before Sam's thoughts were off and running.

What did that really mean? More specifically, what did that mean for *him*? Did God truly have a plan for his life like his grandparents said?

Sam leaned back on the pew as he thought about his friend Jordan's request to come to San Diego. As tempting as it sounded, Sam realized now it wasn't the right thing for him. He needed to do something with his life.

If he only knew what.

He thought of men who had chosen not to go to college and where their lives had taken them and vice versa. There were success stories on both sides, but he couldn't deny there were more successes on the college side.

Since he had become friends with Katie, Sam didn't mind school as much, but he still couldn't get past the idea that maybe, just maybe, he was wasting his time when he could be building a career somewhere else.

Why did life have to get so hard after high school? He still wanted to play. Be a kid. Was that what his dad was doing? Skipping out on responsibilities and still being a kid? Somehow being a kid didn't look so good on a grown-up.

There was a lot of truth to what his grandpa said. He also knew that his grandpa was right about the credit-card debt. He just wasn't sure he was ready to surrender the card—yet. He liked having the freedom it afforded. His grandpa's words immediately came back to him: "Freedom comes with a high price."

Sam sighed and fidgeted in his seat until Emily looked at him and frowned.

If only he knew what the future held for him. If only he could make a decision and stick with it. One minute he was sure a job was the right thing, and the next minute, he was sure college was the right thing. Why didn't life come with a manual?

This time his grandma's voice came to his mind. "The Bible is God's Word, our manual for life and how to live it."

Like it or not, they had affected him with their teachings. And from what he could see in their lives, it worked. Maybe he just needed some time to think it all through—without interruption. That's what he'd do. He'd go somewhere this afternoon where he could be alone and think it through. That was his goal.

By tomorrow, he'd make his decision one way or the other, to quit or stay in school.

AFTER SIPPING COFFEE with cinnamon creamer, reading through devotions together, and sharing in prayer,

Hannah and Charlotte visited a spa. Charlotte had no idea what to expect and was a tad nervous about it. But Hannah had gone to the trouble to schedule them and she was so excited about it, how could Charlotte refuse?

Once they arrived, they were immediately escorted to a back room where the lights were dim and shadows settled in quiet corners. The earthy scent of sandalwood lifted from an incense burner, filling the air with calm. A ruffle of chamomile tea bags feathered the base of a carafe filled with hot water.

"If you ladies will walk this way, I'll take you to your massage room," the lady said.

Charlotte and Hannah shared a glance and then followed the small woman with the pleasant smile back to a private room. There was no doubt in Charlotte's mind that she was out of her element here.

"Just relax and let your worries fade away," Hannah suggested to Charlotte.

"Okay, I'll try," Charlotte agreed. Surely she could let herself be pampered and enjoy it. She decided to allow herself this moment to let her cares slip away.

In what felt like the blink of an eye Charlotte was jolted from the dream world back to the here and now. How long had she been sleeping? A thin veil of haze wrapped around her brain. A sweeping glance around the room was blurred. When she slipped off the table, her legs felt like cooked spaghetti.

If she stayed on that table, she could easily sleep like a baby for a good twelve hours.

"Did I not tell you it would be wonderful?" Hannah said with one look at her.

"Yes, you did. That was heavenly."

They laughed together, gathering their things as they took a moment to regroup.

Charlotte and Hannah edged toward the door to leave the spa when Charlotte's massage therapist stopped them. "Charlotte, are you driving home?"

"No, why?"

"You look a little too relaxed to be behind the wheel," the therapist said with a chuckle.

"You should have a sign that says, 'Don't massage and drive,'" Hannah said.

The two friends shoved out the door, feeling better than they had in months.

"I have to say that was utterly incredible," Charlotte said.

"Didn't I tell you?" Hannah had a bounce in her step, but Charlotte just wanted to curl up in bed.

Charlotte ambled along the sidewalk, her vision adjusting to the rich colors of summer around her, the lush lawns, enormous flower tubs bursting with color and variety. Though a bright sun dazzled above them, the relentless heat had eased, making the walk comfortable. A slight breeze lifted the aroma of honey-roasted peanuts as they passed a little shop that specialized in the tasty treat.

"Did you know they have an apple festival here in September every year?" Hannah asked.

"I've heard about that, but never have been."

"We should come back to it! Just walk around in the fresh September air, drink in the tart scent of apples." Hannah closed her eyes and with a smile took a deep breath, murmuring "Hmm" on the exhale.

"Sounds good to me."

"Did I ever tell you my grandparents had an apple orchard when I was growing up?" Hannah asked.

"No, you didn't." Charlotte was amazed at all she didn't know about her friend. Seemed a weekend getaway was a good time to open up with friends.

"Well, they did. Every year, I helped my nanny—that's what I called Grandma—make applesauce. We'd boil the apples till they reached peak tenderness, and then we'd grind them through a sieve to take off the skins. Nanny always made a batch with red hot candies thrown in for me." She lifted a pleasurable sigh. "I miss those days with my nanny."

Charlotte thought about that and hoped her grandchildren would have special memories with her when they grew up. Sometimes they got so caught up in the daily grind of living, she forgot to stop and make memories. She made a mental note to make more of an effort with that. Maybe take Emily shopping, watch a movie with Sam, play a game with Christopher. They did those things from time to time, but she'd make more of a conscious effort from here on out before time slipped away from them.

"That's wonderful that you have those memories, Hannah."

"Yeah. I think that's why the fall is my favorite time of year. Because it makes me think of Nanny and Papaw."

Charlotte smiled. She had visions of her brother Chet and her running around at her own grandparents' farm. How she missed Chet. Some days she couldn't imagine that he was already in heaven.

So important to make the most of the days we are given.

"Well, you ready for that manicure and pedicure?" Hannah said with a twinkle in her eye.

Charlotte nodded like a giddy teenager.

"Our boys won't know us when we get home."

Laughter filled the air as the two friends headed for their next adventure, making the most of their time together.

"WHAT ARE YOU DOING out here?" Emily asked, joining Sam on the porch after Sunday lunch.

Sam shook himself from his tangle of thoughts and said, "Just thinking."

"Do you want me to leave?"

"No. Come on over and sit down." He nodded toward the seat beside him. He was actually grateful for the reprieve. His brain practically rattled from all the thinking he had done today over his future. "I hear you're quite the hero."

"I wouldn't call it that." Her face was sober and pinched.

"What's wrong? I would think you'd be happy that you were able to help Will," Sam said.

"Yes, of course I'm thrilled he's okay. It's just that I keep thinking how I put up such a stink over going to that babysitting class, but, if I hadn't gone, Will could be . . . dead today."

Sam thought a moment. "Yeah, that's pretty heavy stuff." His gaze swept across the lawn. "But the good news is you did take it and Will is fine, thanks to you."

She lifted a weak smile. "Yeah, that's true." She hesitated.

"The other thing is I was on the computer when he ate that grape. I should have been watching him better."

"Those things happen, Em. Moms keep an eye on their kids, but they have to do other things, too. They can't stare at them 24/7."

"I guess. But moms seem to have eyes in the backs of their heads."

He laughed. "I guess that's true."

"I've never been more scared in my life, Sam."

"I understand that, believe me, after losing that kid at the day care. There are no words to describe what goes on in your head at a time like that or the panic that slices through you."

"Exactly." Emily looked grateful that he understood.

Sometimes his siblings drove him crazy, but he truly loved them both. He reached over and put his arm around Emily. "I'm proud of you, Sis."

"Thanks."

Sam pulled away and kicked the swing slightly into action.

"So what are you thinking about?"

"Just trying to decide where I want to go from here."

A flicker of sadness shadowed Emily's face.

"Don't worry. I'm not leaving just yet."

She frowned. "But someday. We all will one day, and I don't like to think about that. I want us all to stay together."

"I know."

Once their mother died, the three of them had clung to each other with a deep bond that many siblings never know. All they had at that point was each other.

"Are you thinking about what to do after college?" she asked.

"No." He looked at the door to make sure no one was listening. "I've been thinking more about whether I want to stay in college."

She looked surprised. "Why wouldn't you?"

He shrugged. "Just not sure if it's for me."

The porch swing creaked beneath their weight, the chains squeaking with the movement.

"Jordan wants me to come to San Diego," he said quietly.

Emily gasped.

He turned to her. "Shh, Grandma and Grandpa don't know."

"You're thinking about it?" Panic lit her eyes.

"I was. But I'm not leaning that way so much now. It sounds fun, but not really practical. I guess I have to learn to be responsible now whether I like the idea or not."

Emily took a calming breath. Her shoulders relaxed and the tension in her face eased. "College can take you more places than high school can."

"That's what I hear."

"But you don't agree?"

"I'm not saying that. I see success stories on both sides. I'm just trying to figure out where I fit in."

"I get it."

"Do you want to go to college?" he asked.

"Yes. I'd like to work toward some sort of fashion degree. Sure can't get that in high school."

"Girls. They always seem to know what they want."

Emily chuckled. "I think it's more of an individual thing rather than a gender thing."

"Maybe."

"Well, whatever you decide, I hope it keeps you here for a few more years." Emily shoved off the porch swing. "Grandma will be coming home this evening. I sure miss her."

Sam smiled. "Me too."

DYLAN'S MOM dropped Christopher off at the farm after lunch. He walked up toward the porch where Sam sat on the swing.

"Hey," he said.

"Hey, yourself. Why the long face?" Sam asked.

Christopher paused, not sure if he wanted his brother to know. Then he decided to risk it.

He settled on the swing beside his brother. "I think Bailey's mad at me and I have no idea why."

Sam grinned. "Let me give you some advice, little brother. We will never understand the ways of women."

That advice didn't help him all that much.

"So what happened?"

Christopher told Sam about last night, nothing eventful that he could remember. Lastly, he mentioned her comment about the dance.

"Ah, stop right there," Sam said.

Christopher blinked. "What is it?"

"She wants you to take her to the dance."

"What?" Christopher felt broadsided. "I don't know how to dance." There was a shriek to his voice, and he was glad none of his friends heard him.

"Calm down. She doesn't care if you dance or not. She just wants to be asked. That's all."

"I can't do it," Christopher said.

"Okay, then don't. I'm just telling you that's the trouble."

Sam looked as though he thought this was amusing, but Christopher didn't see anything funny about it at all.

"Well, I'm not going to some stupid dance with a girl," Christopher said, standing to his feet with purpose.

"Okay then. Just so you don't mind if she goes with someone else," Sam slipped in.

Christopher thought a minute. "I don't mind." With that, he turned and walked into the house, instantly feeling better.

It felt good to know what the problem was and how to handle it. He also discovered another important thing: he wasn't ready for a girlfriend yet.

Chapter
Twenty-Eight

C harlotte's heart gave a jump when she spotted the farm. Only gone three days and it was a very welcome sight.

"Hannah, I can't thank you enough for taking me along on your trip. It has been such fun," Charlotte said, gathering her handbag and pulling it onto her lap.

"And to think you almost didn't come with me."

Charlotte shook her head. "I would have missed out on so much. This has been the best decision I've made in a very long time."

Hannah smiled and turned her car into the driveway at Charlotte's house.

"The truth is I wouldn't have let you say no. I was taking you with me if I had to drag you and stuff you in my suitcase." She laughed.

"Oh, dear," Charlotte said. "I'm glad you didn't have to do that."

Hannah popped open the trunk. She got out with Charlotte and lifted the suitcase to her.

"Thanks, friend." Charlotte put the suitcase on the ground and gave Hannah a long hug. "Don't know what I'd do without you, neighbor."

"Same here. God is good."

Charlotte pulled away, looked at her friend, and said, "All the time."

Just then the front screen door slammed open.

"Grandma!" Christopher came running to her side and gave her a big hug.

"Well, looks as though you've been missed," Hannah said with a wide grin. "I wonder if my man will give me the same greeting."

Hannah got back inside her car and backed out while Christopher and Charlotte waved.

With her arm around Christopher's shoulder, Charlotte and her grandson turned to head toward the front porch just as other family members clustered around the door.

"Okay, make way," Bob said, scooting everyone aside so Charlotte could get through.

The sight of everyone hovering and anxiously waiting for her warmed Charlotte clear through. She hoped they missed more than her cooking.

"Well, hello," she said, stepping into the house and into outstretched arms—Bob first and then the kids.

"Hey, Grandma, I went to game night with the teens—"

Emily cut off Christopher. "You wouldn't believe what happened while I was babysitting—"

Sam cut off Emily. "When you get a chance, I'd like to talk to you about school."

"Whoa. Now everybody slow down and give your grandma a chance to catch her breath," Bob said, coming to her rescue.

She chuckled. "Well, it sure is nice to know I was missed."

"Here, let me take that." Bob reached over and lifted the luggage from her hand. "I'll just take it to the bedroom for you to sort through later."

"Oh no. I need you to take it to the family room for me, if you would, please."

Bob raised his eyebrows, and then shrugged and complied.

"Thank you, honey." She turned to the kids. "How about we go into the family room. I purchased a few things."

The kids' eyes lit up. No matter the age, everyone liked to be remembered with a gift.

Charlotte looked around the room at the familiar surroundings and breathed deeply of the flickering candle nearby that raised the scent of cinnamon into the room.

"I thought you might like that," Emily said when she spotted Charlotte looking at the candle.

"I love it. Thank you, Emily." Charlotte was beginning to think she should go away more often.

Charlotte settled on the sofa and everyone else found a seat. She couldn't help noticing Christopher was right next to her, not wanting to miss anything. She had to stop herself from laughing.

"Now, don't look for a minute," she said, before she clicked open her suitcase.

The kids looked away. She pulled a large bag from within the compartment and then clicked her luggage shut once more.

"Okay, let's see what we've got here."

"Can we look now?" Christopher asked.

"Yes."

The kids turned to her. She noted that even Bob was watching with interest.

She dug into her bag and pulled out Christopher's item first. Then she turned to him. "You may not need this yet, but it might come in handy one day." She gave him a wrapped gift.

He tore into it with a vengeance. Some things never changed. Once unwrapped, he found a straight razor.

His eyes grew wide and he grinned. "Hey, this is great. Thanks, Grandma!"

Chuckles floated around the room.

She was pleased that Christopher took their teasing good-naturedly.

"This is for you, too, since you can't use the other one yet." She pulled out a Cornhuskers ball cap.

"Awesome. Thanks, Grandma." He reached over and gave her a hug.

"You're welcome. If they'd had one for Sam's school, I would have gotten that one instead. Maybe he can get you one later."

Sam smiled and nodded.

"It's great." Christopher shaped it with his hands and tugged it on.

Everyone told him how good it looked and then Charlotte dug into her bag once again.

"Emily, you're growing up so fast, and I know our tastes aren't always the same, but the young girl in the shop assured me that you would love this." Charlotte gave her a large package.

In no time, Emily found a cute handbag made of denim.

It had plenty of room and had a strap she could sling across her shoulder.

"Oh, I love it, Grandma! Thanks."

Another hug.

"Well, it seems like Christmas around here," Bob said with a tentative grin. No doubt he was a bit worried about the money involved.

"I got good bargains on every item," Charlotte assured him.

Bob settled back into his seat and took a satisfied breath.

"Here's your gift, Sam." She handed it to him.

When he opened the package, he found a cool book bag made of canvas that he could strap to his back and carry around campus. The one he currently used was worn and tattered. He was glad he hadn't purchased a new one with his credit card.

"Thanks, Grandma." He reached over and gave her a hug.

"Hope you kids enjoy your things." She turned to Bob. "Now, I have one for you." She pulled the last item from the bag. It was a nice black and red checkered flannel shirt for working on the farm in the fall weather.

"This is nice. Thanks, Char."

Charlotte watched as her family tried out their new presents and she told them about her time with Hannah, the spa, the manicure/pedicure, skimming the main details.

"You know, since we've all been a bit scattered this weekend, how about we reserve tomorrow evening for family time? We can play games, watch a movie, or just sit around and talk. I think it would be nice to be together. Would you be up for it?" She looked toward her family, hopeful.

Evidently, seeing how much she wanted this, they decided to humor her, because the kids agreed to it.

"Oh, that's wonderful," Charlotte said, sitting back against the sofa. "So is everyone ready for school tomorrow?"

Nods all around.

"I made our lunches so you wouldn't have to do it when you got home," Emily said.

Charlotte shared a glance with Bob, who was smiling.

"That was very considerate of you, Emily. Thank you." She smiled.

"So what happened here while I was gone? Anything fun or interesting?" Charlotte asked.

"I decided me and Bailey are just going to be friends," Christopher said.

"Oh?" She shared another glance with Bob.

"Yeah. She wanted me to go to some dumb dance. I don't like any girl that bad."

They all laughed. Emily rolled her eyes.

Charlotte was greatly relieved to hear that, but she wisely kept it to herself. "Well, you have plenty of time to worry about that. Still, I hope you and Bailey will stay friends. She seems like a very nice girl."

"Yeah, I want to be her friend. After all, I broke her wrist."

Charlotte gasped.

Christopher looked surprised. "I didn't mean—I mean, well, not on purpose, but—"

"She gets it, you goof," Sam said, giving him a nudge.

"You don't know this yet, but we have a hero in our midst," Bob said.

"Oh?" Charlotte said.

"That's right. Emily, why don't you tell her the story?"

Emily looked as though she didn't want to talk about it, but she took a deep breath and proceeded to tell how she helped Will when he was choking. Charlotte hung on to every word, wondering what she herself might have done in such a situation.

"Emily, that is amazing. I don't know that I could have handled it with such calm expertise. I am truly amazed." Charlotte hugged her again. Instead of enjoying her moment, Emily seemed to be holding back. Charlotte could feel it in the hug. She didn't want to talk to her about it in front of everyone so she made a mental note to talk to Emily later.

A girl who saved a life should feel good about it. So why didn't Emily?

⌣ Chapter
Twenty-Nine

Monday afternoon Sam sat down at the computer and checked his eBay offerings. He had some nibbles on a couple of them and one of them had sold at a good price. He liked the idea of selling some of his things to pay off his bills and get his life back in order.

He clicked over to e-mail and then opened the note from Jordan. After reading through it once more, Sam hit the reply icon and began to type.

> *Hey, Jordan, thanks for the invite, dude. But the truth is I've decided to stick it out with school. It seems to be the right thing for me at this point. Now once finals get here, I may change my mind.*
>
> *Later, dude.*

After he clicked out of e-mail, he glanced once more at his eBay posts, and then turned off the computer. Reaching into the drawer of the desk, he pulled out his grandma's scissors and made his way up the stairs to his room. Things suddenly seemed so clear.

He closed the door behind him, walked across the floor, and picked up his wallet from the nightstand. The smell of leather reminded him of yet another purchase he didn't need. Pulling out his Visa card, he shoved it between the scissors and whacked away.

He knew the card wasn't the problem. The problem was him. He didn't have the willpower to handle it yet. Maybe one day, when he got his life back under control, he'd try it again. Then again, maybe he'd leave it alone altogether. In the meantime, he planned to save his money, go to school, and make something of himself.

The plastic card fell to the floor in tiny slivers. He scooped them up and threw them in the trash.

From now on, he'd pay with cash or do without.

That was the plan.

ONCE BOB GOT HOME and they'd had dinner, Charlotte settled with Bob and the kids in the family room. Rain pattered on the rooftop and made wet drops down their windowpanes while the kids chattered on about school. A low growl of thunder rumbled. Charlotte thought it a perfect night for family togetherness.

"So what's your pleasure, a movie, a game, more talking, what?" Charlotte asked the kids.

"How about we play charades?" Christopher asked.

Emily rolled her eyes. "We always play that."

"What would you suggest, Emily?" Bob asked.

She thought a moment, but before she could come up with an answer, someone knocked at the door.

"Hold that thought." Charlotte walked toward the front door, wondering who it could be on a Monday evening.

Hannah and Frank huddled beneath an oversized umbrella. "I told Frank you were probably sick of me by now, but he wanted to come over and visit."

"You are always welcome here, and you know it," Charlotte said, stepping aside to let them in.

Hannah shook the water from her umbrella and leaned it against the porch wall before stepping inside.

"I've been so busy, I just needed a break in the routine and wanted to visit with our good friends," Frank said.

They walked into the family room and Bob got up to greet them. They exchanged a few greetings and just as Charlotte bent down to sit on the sofa, another knock sounded at the door.

"Want me to get it, Grandma?" Emily asked.

"No, honey. I'll get it." Her knees protested, but she ignored them again. Once she got to the door, she was surprised to see Bill, Anna, and the girls standing there. Bill was holding a large sheet cake. "What in the world? Is it someone's birthday?"

"No, nothing like that. We never got a chance to thank Emily properly, so we thought we would bring a cake to celebrate." Bill grinned, lifting the cake. "And you know how Anna refuses to go anywhere on a school night. But actually, this was her idea."

"Well, by all means, come in," Charlotte said.

The family stepped inside. Amid the hubbub of the company greetings, Charlotte felt a rush of warmth spread through her for this special time together.

"Well, look what the wind blew in," Bob said when he saw the kids.

"At least it blew some cake in with us." Bill lifted the sugared treat.

"Did I forget something?" Bob wanted to know. "Is this a party for someone?"

Bill explained again that they wanted to celebrate Emily's heroics. Charlotte noted the bloom of pink in Emily's cheeks. She had finally learned the full story of what had happened when Will choked—how Emily had been on the computer—and she knew Emily was still suffering guilt over it.

Anna walked over to Emily. "I'm sorry I reacted the way I did the other day, Emily. I still don't want you on the computer while you're babysitting, mind you, but I'm very proud of the way you handled the situation. Your uncle reminded me of a few things I'd done when I was your age, and I realized I was too harsh with you. I'm sorry." She gave Emily a light hug.

"Thank you," Emily said, looking quite astounded.

Soon the family room burst with chatter while Charlotte and Hannah carried the cake into the kitchen and set to work cutting up pieces and placing them on dessert plates for everyone.

Pete and Dana shoved through the back door, surprising the women in the kitchen.

"What on earth—" Hannah turned around.

Charlotte put her hands on her hips and looked at Pete. "I might have known you'd smell the dessert."

He laughed. "You know it. Try to have some without me, will ya?"

Dana shook her head.

Charlotte explained what was going on and Pete and Dana quickly drifted into the family room with the others.

"So it sounds like there was a little excitement here while we were gone," Hannah said, lifting another dessert plate to Charlotte.

"It would appear so."

"Are you sorry that you went after all?" Hannah looked at her.

"Not in the least."

Hannah relaxed and lifted a smile. "I'm glad."

"They obviously did fine without me," Charlotte said.

"But I'm sure they wouldn't want you to make a practice of being gone," Hannah said.

"Oh, I'm sure of that. Who would do the laundry?"

They laughed together while everyone shuffled into the kitchen.

"I would like to say the prayer," Bill announced as hushes rippled around the room.

"Go right ahead," Bob said.

"Lord, we thank You for this very special moment in time that You've given us to spend together. We honor You and we thank You for working through Emily to save our boy." His voice stuck on the last sentence. A moment of silence followed.

Charlotte brushed a tear from her eye and heard the sniffles around the room.

"We thank You, Lord, for Your grace and mercy. And we thank You that Emily was faithful with her gifts and skills and put them to use for such a time as this. Oh, and thank you for the cake. Amen."

Charlotte's heart warmed at seeing her family rally around Emily this way. She glanced out the window. The rain had stopped, taking with it the uncomfortable heat. Charlotte suggested they go out on the porch with the cake, coffee, and tea.

A bright moon sailed over the treetops, while a slight breeze whispered through tree limbs, causing leaves to shake off excess raindrops. The very slight chill in the air gave the hint that summer was coming to an end and Charlotte imagined the scent of ripe, crisp apples.

She stepped back against the porch railing, watching the interaction of her family and dear friends.

A perfect moonlit night, surrounded by family and friends. A night of celebration.

Pete came up beside his mom and put his hand on her shoulder. "You okay?"

"I'm fine." She smiled.

"They're turning out all right, Mom. You and Dad should feel good about that," he said.

"It's not our doing. They're making good choices."

"Yeah, and your prayers and guidance are helping that, I'm sure."

Charlotte started to protest, but Pete held out his hand. "Hey, look how good I turned out."

Without skipping a beat, Charlotte said, "Like I said, it's not our doing."

They laughed together.

Sam stepped inside and then came right back out. "Hey, Christopher," he called out.

Everyone turned around.

"You've got a phone call. It's a girl. She says she's some friend from school. Morgan somebody."

Bill and Pete let out catcalls until Charlotte gave them "the look."

"It appears our boy is growing up," Bob said, slipping up beside Charlotte and putting his arm around her.

"I don't like the idea of girls calling boys," she said with a frown.

"It's a new day."

She sighed. "Think we'll make it through the growing pains?"

"I know we will, Charlotte. With the Lord on our side, we can make it through anything."

She smiled and snuggled into his arms. "You're right, Bob. You're so right."

With the breeze stirring through their hair, while the moments slipped into memories, Charlotte and Bob stood embracing beneath a moonlit sky and whispered a prayer of gratitude for good friends, for one another, and for the children who had changed their lives in a wonderful way.

About the Author

D iann Hunt was the award-winning author of numerous novels and novellas. An Indiana native, she passed away in 2013.

A Note from the Editors

We hope you enjoyed this volume in the Home to Heather Creek series, published by Guideposts. For over seventy-five years, Guideposts, a non-profit organization, has been driven by a vision of a world filled with hope. We aspire to be the voice of a trusted friend, a friend who makes you feel more hopeful and connected.

By making a purchase from Guideposts, you join our community in touching millions of lives, inspiring them to believe that all things are possible through faith, hope, and prayer. Your continued support allows us to provide uplifting resources to those in need.

Whether through our online communities, websites, apps, or publications, we strive to inspire our audiences, bring them together, and comfort, uplift, entertain, and guide them.

To learn more, please go to guideposts.org.

Find inspiration, find faith, find Guideposts.

Shop our best sellers and favorites at
guideposts.org/shop

Or scan the QR code to go directly to our Shop